Saving Seniors' Savings

Best Kept Secrets on How to Pay for Senior Services

Therese Johnson

Saving Seniors' Savings: Best Kept Secrets on How to Pay for Senior Services Copyright © 2017 by Therese Johnson.

On all legal matters, consult with an appropriate legal professional.

On all medical matters, consult with an appropriate medical or mental health professional. The authors of this book cannot and do not provide legal or medical advice, and the contents of this book are not professional legal or medical advice. Where information is provided that may have some bearing on medical, mental health, and legal issues, it is not an independent tool for diagnostics, for treatment, or for legal conclusions about any of the issues discussed. While the authors have sought to provide useful information on the matters discussed in this book, ongoing research and development constantly changes our understanding of medical and mental health issues, and various medical and mental health professionals may have differing views from that in this book. The authors are not attorneys at law and cannot and do not dispense legal advice, and laws and regulations vary from jurisdiction to jurisdiction, from agency to agency, and they change from time to time. Always consult with appropriate professionals on all matters.

Published by Prominence Publishing: www.prominencepublishing.com

To learn more about the author Therese Johnson, please contact:
www.seniorcareofsacramento.com
Email: seniorcareofsacramento@gmail.com
Telephone: 916-877-6904

ISBN: 978-1-988925-00-4

What People Are Saying…

"We desperately needed assistance in finding the right place for my mother and father-in-law. The list of possible scenarios was endless and totally frustrating. Questions like should they be in a nursing home or assisted living? What areas are available to us in our price range? Do they need a registered nurse to be on site? What benefits are available? Nobody I talked to was able to answer these questions UNTIL we were referred by Rick Buckman at the Veterans office to Therese Johnson…From the first phone consult, she was caring & knowledgeable, and open to our particular situation. She has followed through in finding the perfect place where all their needs are being met by friendly professional caregivers. We highly recommend Therese Johnson as a senior care consultant and are open to anyone contacting us for more information."

--Jane Jennings

"Your diligence to your work is an amazing thing to see in this day we live in. You should be proud of your commitment to your clients. The assistance you provided to our mom as well as to my sister and I have given us such peace of mind. I

would like to personally THANK YOU for not only the knowledge and service you provided, but for being there for my mom when the tears were flowing and you knew all the right words to say."

--Jeri Evans

"Senior Care of Sacramento answered all our questions about senior living options. They were able to narrow down the list quickly to zero in on the most appropriate facilities to meet our needs. For example, they helped us to consider all the pros and cons of moving our loved one to a residential care home versus a large retirement home environment.

Therese Johnson heads Senior Care of Sacramento. She has a list of qualifications a mile long and really knows her business. She advocates planning ahead because you can not make these decisions at the last minute. You would be overwhelmed. She charges a consultation fee and it is worth every penny. And, not only that, if you use her placement services, the fee is refundable.

Therese is a gold-mine of knowledge about senior care. She goes above and beyond to find the right fit and she is a staunch advocate of every type of help and assistance that seniors need. Too much to list here. We were so impressed we wanted others in our situation to know there is good professional help available to figure out where, when and how to choose an appropriate senior living arrangement."

-- Jennifer T., Seattle Washington

Additional video testimonials are available on our website at www.seniorcareofsacramento.com.

Dedication

I want to dedicate this book to the two most influential important women in my life and who suffered with dementia.

My beloved mother, Shirley Matthews, was a Registered Nurse for over 45 years who always encouraged me to become anything in the world I wanted to be. She has been suffering with dementia for 8 years and was recently put on hospice.

My recently deceased mother-in-law, Jean Harmon, was also a Registered Nurse for over 45 years. I adored her; she was an amazing mentor who never ceased to inspire and entertain me with her incredible wit and intellect.

In Gratitude

I want to thank my wonderful editor Valerie Kack. Without her, this work would not have been the same. Thank you Valerie for your encouragement, support and guidance.

I want to thank my husband Walter Johnson for his continuous help during this endeavor and for providing me the love and foundation I needed so that I could complete this work and for always being my stable rock in holding down the fort when I was absent and doing research. This book truly would not have come to fruition if it weren't for him. So many thanks my love.

Foreword

Although I have traveled around the world, I have spent all of my life living in America. I am very proud of my country for a number of reasons, but one of the things we do not do well is honor and respect our elderly.

As a blind person myself, I realize I am part of a minority group as are people with various religious and ethnic characteristics; however, one minority we will all be a part of, unless we die young, is that of a senior citizen.

I have been blessed to have a number of mentors in my personal and professional life. Among them were legendary coach John Wooden and Hall-of-Fame broadcaster Paul Harvey. Both of these gentlemen were high-functioning individuals and extraordinary contributors to society well into their 90s. My father ran a retirement center and nursing home for many years and only retired, himself, in his 80s. My parents now live in the retirement center/nursing home that my father ran for several decades. That experience allowed me to see, first hand, the high quality of life that is available as a senior citizen provided that there is some forethought and planning.

Like most things in life, living well through your Golden Years just doesn't happen by itself. We need to plan financially, emotionally, and in every other way for ourselves and those that we care about. In this book Therese Johnson has given us all a lot to think about and a roadmap for reaching our destination of a happy, healthy, and productive retirement.

As the Baby Boomers begin to retire in unprecedented numbers, they have more opportunities and resources than any previous generation. If you reach retirement age today without some sort of debilitating disease, you have a good possibility of living into your second century. The fastest-growing demographic group in America is made up of centenarians. Many of these 100-year-old individuals are not simply incoherent shells of their former selves. They are active, engaged, and productive members of their families and our society.

As the author of over 40 books, I'm often doing research. When I think about the Great Depression or the period between the two world wars, I don't have to research that period from a book. I can pick up the phone and call any number of people who lived through that time.

You and I may literally live a third of our lives beyond retirement. It, therefore, behooves us to take advantage of every opportunity and resource to make those years not simply a time of surviving but a time of thriving.

I wish you health and happiness throughout a long and fruitful life.

Jim Stovall

2017

TABLE OF CONTENTS

Introduction

I wrote this book to guide aging seniors and families through the process of creating a custom long-term care plan that allows them to be able to afford in-home or residential caregiving, and protects real estate and other assets from government liens. I will guide you through the morass of confusion. You will discover the three or four programs that are optimally suited for your specific situation. You will know which government programs are dysfunctional and must be avoided completely. You will know, without doubt, how to rearrange your income and assets to be in exactly the right position to qualify for getting most or all of your senior care expenses paid for by the three or four programs to which I point you.

I am also writing this with the hopes of saving my time and energy and the time and energy of those I serve. In an effort to answer my clients' questions and reduce repeating myself to those I serve who seek the resources and methods of acquiring available senior services, I am presenting this material to assist them in a guide format for them to follow so I can hand this to prospective clients and our first meetings can be informed and take less time.

My goal is to provide this simple book to seniors who likely have no idea what is available in their search to remain independent, and who hope to pass on their savings and assets to their family members. Families will benefit from a customized plan for their medical care, nursing care, or other caregiving needs and support when their aging loved one needs services. When it is time to call me for resource or placement guidance, this step will save us all time, energy and money.

It is unfortunate but many of the government programs designed to help seniors are so dysfunctional and overloaded with bureaucratic red tape that it takes a professional to weed through their policies and procedures to get applications for these benefit programs processed. This book offers resources for determining or acquiring eligibility, and for some individuals, may assist in actually getting benefits. Being prepared for this process helps manage the feelings of helplessness or powerlessness when facing the kinds of decisions involved with assisting an aging loved one.

Chapter One

What Do I Know?

How did I get into this business as a long-term care (LTC) consultant? Let me tell you a little about myself so that you know I am speaking from experience so you can be comfortable in knowing that I know what I'm talking about.

Originally, I went to college to become a lawyer. I know, "Right?" Don't put the book down yet. When my mentor/professor quoted an anecdote from Plato that the sign of a sick society was one with too many doctors and lawyers, I decided to go into a more nurturing profession, and I went into healthcare instead.

I did my internship in college working for some Senators and Assemblymen, and on their staff, promoting advocacy for Senior Issues which had to do with safety and fraud awareness targeted at seniors. I also put on a very successful women's self-defense workshop for California Assemblyman Phil Isenberg who was once the Mayor of Sacramento.

I went on to marry and have a large family. It wouldn't be until ten years later that I found myself once again advocating for seniors. But this time it wasn't just for safety, it was for the right to be able to choose the level of care a senior needed in our healthcare system. To have a choice in their care options was the greatest challenge because some kinds of placements were being denied by insurance companies.

I graduated with degrees in Government and Gerontology after taking Nursing courses and certifications, and working as a certified nurse in acute care hospitals and skilled nursing hospitals. But a divorce left me with five children to support on my own. I applied for an Administrator's license to open a six-bed Residential Care Facility for the Elderly (RCFE) also called Assisted Living (ASL) or Board and Care. I managed to acquire my RCFE license in 3 months… thanks to my experience working in government and with the legislature. I took a Nursing job at a local Skilled Nursing Facility (SNF) to make sure I was really up for the challenge of owning and operating an RCFE. After nine months working at a SNF, it was clear to me I could provide a better quality of care for seniors than a SNF. So my RCFE came to be in the early 1990's.

I opened the RCFE, and joined a local Care Home Owners' networking group, called "Foothill Care Providers for the Elderly" or F.A.C.E.S. With a colleague, I started a crusade with other members of FACES to change the MediCal or Medicaid law that gave low-income seniors no choice but SNF placements, even if their level of healthcare made them eligible to reside at an RCFE. Thus, began our 7-year journey together to get a new law passed that allowed low-income MediCal or Medicaid seniors to be able to move to RCFE's if their health care level deemed them eligible. We proved to the California legislature, that it was going to save taxpayers $42,000,000 a month, in addition to giving seniors freedom to choose a higher quality of care. So after five years, we got the law passed in 2000 but it was implemented poorly as "The Assisted Living Waiver Pilot Project," otherwise known as the ALWP. This project is currently only open in ten counties in California for a total of approximately 2,000-3,000 residents statewide.

Until such time as our Department of Health Services and Department of Social Services who govern SNF and RCFE licensing requirements are able to open up the program statewide to California, and elsewhere, as a Federal program, so that all low-income seniors can take advantage of the ALW (as the program is now called) program, and save California taxpayers millions of dollars. Still, only a miniscule number of seniors are being allowed the use of this taxpayer saving benefit, and quality of life choice.

The way the ALW saves taxpayers money and helps low-income seniors is to allow seniors who need assistance with activities of daily living (ADL), such as bathing, dressing, grooming, medication management, transportation, housekeeping, meals etc., but who don't need expensive nursing, doctor oversight or supervision to be admitted to an RCFE, instead of a SNF, or to be able to stay at home and pay for an In-Home caregiver. Currently, MediCal or Medicaid will only pay for SNF long-term care for low-income seniors at rates of $6,000 to $15,000 a month depending on their level of care. Considering that many of these same seniors are eligible for RCFE care at the rates of $2,000 to $5,000 a month in a non-institutional hospital setting with a higher quality environment and care, we are not doing ourselves any favors by not allowing RCFE and home care more affordable options to everyone.

To see more about the ALW or to apply for one of their county low-income help programs go to:

http://www.dhcs.ca.gov/services/ltc/Pages/AssistedLivingW aiver.aspxw

Upon closing my RCFE I went to work for a local nurse registry and worked at most of the local hospitals to get familiar with them to see which one I wanted to work for permanently. I ended up choosing the hospital closest to my home. I worked there for 3 years; 2 years on their surgical floor and 1 year in their telemetry and Intensive Care Units (ICU) units. Soon enough, I was disillusioned with the hospital's policies and procedures for nurses as they assigned me too many patients on a regular basis and when I complained, they deemed me a trouble-maker. I had to have the union represent me in my concerns for patient safety on several occasions.

Ultimately, I was offered a position as a consultant with an established Senior Care Placement and Referral Service which had been the first referral and placement service in the Sacramento area, and had been in business for 13 years, so I took the position and quit the hospital. I loved working as a Senior Care consultant and when the company dissolved after I had been there a few years, I opened up my own Senior Care Consulting company, "Senior Care of Sacramento," (SCOS) with the support and encouragement of my husband.

I have experience working at all 3 levels of care: a SNF, Acute Care Hospitals, and owned and operated my own RCFE. In addition to working as an advocate for seniors with the California State Legislature and Board of Registered Nurses, and while I was operating my RCFE and advocating for MediCal or Medicaid Reform, I started an Alzheimer Research Group and Nursing Education Provider Business for which I still am the President.

If that isn't enough credentials, I also was a Marketing Director for a large 100-bed RCFE owned by a corporation, and for a nurse on-call registry doing In-Home Care for a year. I continued as a legislative advocate and as the FACES community advocate for 7 years. During this time, I trained and became certified as a Hospice volunteer for our local Sutter Hospital Hospice. I offer Reiki treatments to Hospice patients when they request it. Not many people are educated about the many benefits of the ancient Japanese healing technique, Reiki. It is most famous for pain relief and used in many pain, cancer and Hospice clinics.

Chapter Two

Getting Started

SCOS has worked with many different scenarios and much of the work is with the family of the senior. Often, however, we have worked with the senior when they had outlived their loved ones or just did not have anyone else in their life to assist them with their needs. This resource is for anyone seeking support with finding and utilizing resources when seniors are in need.

In order to advise someone correctly and direct them to what resources are available, it is crucial for us to know what their needs and requirements entail. So the first thing that is needed is an assessment of the individual's overall health in the following areas: financial, emotional, physical, mental, and spiritual. This may require medical summaries, physical agility or strength testing, a visit with a psychotherapist or minister, and is best coordinated by an experienced professional such as myself.

This is the first step in determining the needs of the individual seeking assistance. We can create a long term care plan that includes what the future needs might be. We can accurately determine what assistance is needed only after doing this initial assessment. The 3 page assessment form I use can be found at the back of the book under Appendix A. It needs to be completed and returned to me. You can also get it online at: www.SeniorCareofSacramento.com.

Or you can email us the completed information form to SeniorCareofSacramento@gmail.com or fax to 530-823-0646.

We need to know what's most important to you, the senior, and/or the caregiver.

My philosophy and goal as a Gerontologist and as a member of "The National Aging in Place Council" is to keep all seniors in their homes as long as possible.

Generally, we start here if at all possible unless it is not economically feasible or logistically unreasonable. For these reasons, we customize each client's care plan based on their individual care needs, wants, budget, and location. To do this:

A. We need to know: What is most important to you?

Examples of what we need to know:

1. Is staying home your most important priority?
2. Or are you lonely?

3. Do you miss having company because you can't get out or drive anymore?

4. Do you have a beloved pet that you want to keep with you and you are afraid that if you move to assisted living you won't be able to take it with you?

5. Do you want to stay in the same neighborhood as your friends and family but you're not sure you can afford it?

6. Perhaps a priority is your wish to leave an inheritance to your grandchildren, and you don't want all your monies usurped by medical bills?

B. What are your likes and dislikes?

1. What is it about where you live now that makes you happy or fulfills you?

2. What organizations have you belonged to? SIRS, ELKS, ALGP? Soroptomist, Lions?

3. Do you consider yourself of low, middle or upper income? What neighborhood and social status are you accustomed to? Do you identify with a certain kind of person? (We use this information to determine what budget fits which care homes and neighborhoods.)

4. Do you love going to church? Belong to a church or community organization?

5. Do you like to dance? Do you listen to a certain kind of music--jazz, country, big band, rock and roll, classical? Do you prefer to watch television?
6. Do you read? Would you like to be in a book club?
7. Do you like sports? Fishing? Playing cards?
8. Do you like to go to the theater? Do you hate the Opera or love it?
9. What are your food preferences; are you a vegetarian? Do you hate liver or fish?
10. Do you consider yourself a loner (introverted) or needing social connection (extroverted)?

OK, you get the idea! We really do our best at Senior Care of Sacramento to customize a plan that meets as many of your needs and desires as possible. We will create a personalized long-term care plan for you or your loved one so that you can have time for yourself and not just time for the ones you love.

If you are under financial stress we'll help you get the resources you need!

Are you at the point beyond burn-out? We can give you the freedom to get your life back!

C. What's most important to your family and/or caregivers?

Did you know that over 67% of caregivers die before the person they are caring for, due to stress? Do you want to avoid becoming one of these caregiver statistics? We can help you. We have solutions. We can help you get rested, restored and the help you need to stay healthy!

1. Is having more time to yourself a priority in your life right now?
2. Would you like to have a whole day all to yourself, without anyone or anything making any demands on you or your time? Or for that matter would you like to have someone waiting on you for a change? (And by the way you should not feel guilty for wanting these things.)
3. Do you want to have more time with your husband or to travel, take a vacation, visit or spend time with your children or friends?
4. Are you sleep-deprived, physically and emotionally or mentally drained?
5. Are you confused? Don't know what options are available to seniors such as financial resources to help pay for care or caregiver options available for your budget?

6. Do you know what the cost is to you for not getting help with your caregiving demands? We can provide resources and assist with the acquisition of support.

D. How will you know when to ask for help?

First of all, some people never ask for help. They have yet to learn the life lesson of asking for help. I can relate to this as I was raised to be very independent. My mother always told my siblings and I that we were blessed to be living in a world where anything was possible, and that we could grow up to become and do anything we wanted if we set our minds to it. Coming from a woman who grew up as a child during the "Great Depression Era" and who raised 8 children with a gambler for a husband, she really did pretty well for herself and managed to save enough to make her retirement better than most.

When you become a caregiver for someone else, it is essential to consider getting some caregiver relief; that is, help, to make sure you have a day off from caregiving. It is not a job that should be done alone. In our western society, we have gotten away from the concept of the extended family. But in the current economy, the high cost of senior care and healthier life expectancy, it is actually becoming a choice families are making out of necessity. There are three generation families with children and grandparents in the same household, placing a burden on the money-making and caregiving generation, such as daughters and daughters-in-laws who are many times still caring for their own children. We call this "The Sandwich generation".

Unfortunately, the deterioration of family structure is a major issue that is creating havoc on our ability to return to a concept of an "extended family network." This is all the more reason for creating long term care planning for our seniors!

The best way for families to get help is to seek out an expert like Senior Care of Sacramento who can assist in creating a long term care plan for yourself and your loved ones.

I am also providing some tools and information to assist you in determining the costs associated with keeping a loved one at home vs. an RCFE and questions to ask yourself about whether or not it is time to move a loved one or yourself to an RCFE.

I want to give you an example of a senior consulting case I worked on to give you an idea of the multitude of different scenarios that we here at Senior Care of Sacramento have assisted. Here is an example of how we solve a customer's problems:

A 67 year old son was caregiving his 92 year old dad who suffers from kidney failure and needs dialysis 3 times a week, and is also a serious fall risk. His son promised to keep his dad at home so he stays with him 3 weeks a month. When he goes home to his wife (who lives 50 minutes away) one week a month, his sister flies out from the east coast to give her brother a break. The dad's monthly income was $1175.00 and was all going to pay for his 3 weekly dialysis treatments and medications. We were able to get resources for the dad to supplement his monthly income and get his dialysis paid for without using his monthly income. The dad now has an annual income of almost $40,000. With these resources the son can afford to hire a caregiver 35 hours per week, or be able to afford an RCFE if his dad falls again and can't return home.

We get the satisfaction of knowing that we helped make this family's lives easier and more manageable and were able to create a better quality of life for not only the dad, but the whole family.

I have been working in the healthcare industry for over 22 years now. I am personally aware of the different levels of care available to seniors and their loved ones. I have advocated for many individuals and families over the years as a private consultant, nurse and gerontologist, as well as cared for my own beloved mother, who has suffered with dementia for 8 years and my adored mother-in-law who passed away with dementia several years ago.

Note: In addition to the intake assessment forms, please use the Comparison Worksheet found in Appendix C to determine the senior's current budget. You will see the comparison of a care facility's amenities vs cost to stay at home with In Home Care to see how placement may in fact save you money.

Chapter Three

Myths about In Home Health Services (IHHS) and RCFE's

Often, families must face the difficult decision that placement in a care facility is best for the loved one, especially when the level of care needed is greater than what the family can provide. However, many seniors are misinformed or uneducated about the current care facility industry. Many have memories of horrific places where their parents or loved ones were placed in the days before the industry was regulated and licensed by the Dept. of Health and the Dept. of Social Services.

These myths must be dispelled in our society and for our seniors. Sometimes the only way of doing that is to tour a facility and by actually allowing a loved one or senior to experience today's better regulated, improved hygiene and a less institutional-like RCFE community environment. There are many quality communities for seniors available to them. The task of seeking the "right" placement can be facilitated by a professional gerontologist and care specialist like me.

17

Many seniors, who remain in their homes, isolate for various reasons. Some have health or incontinence related concerns, others don't hear or see well and can't understand others. Some are too tired, weak, or habitually introverted to reach out. And many don't even consider asking for help. The majority of people and human nature dictates that people are social animals. To isolate and ostracize ourselves from each other is not healthy. We all need affection and companionship to remain healthy and of sound mind and body. Without companionship, some people will wither and die, or go a little crazy.

I have too often seen this to be the case. It is heartbreaking to come upon seniors who have been isolated either by their own doing or by neglect. This is another reason I am writing this book as a resource for seniors to get the help that is available to them. Please give it as a gift if you know someone who is isolated and living alone.

It is unfortunate that with many things in our culture the media reports the negative news more than the positive news. This has contributed to fears in people surrounding RCFE communities, but I assure you there are many more positive aspects of RCFE and Assisted Living communities than negative. We just don't hear about it in the general public, or from the media.

I can assure you from my experience that the positives outweigh the negatives. What do you do when mom and/or dad want to stay at home but they don't think they need any help to do that? One way is to try to dispel some of the myths that surround in home caregivers and care facilities; even the word *caregiver* can trigger a negative reaction.

Another myth is that it is cheaper for someone who needs care to stay at home and get in-home help rather than move to an ASL or RCFE. This is only the case up to a point. It depends on how much help someone needs; how much hands-on assistance they need and how much time they need assistance during the day and/or night; and whether or not they need supervision for safety.

If you have completed the 3 page Assessment Form I discussed in the previous chapter and the comparison sheet for costs of In-Home-Care vs. RCFE, then you perhaps have a little more insight into the cost differences I refer to.

If you have been caring for one or both of your parents or your spouse in your home or theirs, then you likely know how many hours of care they need daily or how much supervision they need. If you are not living with them and not doing the hands-on care, you may not know exactly how much time and care is required for them or how much supervision they actually need for safety. If your loved one has dementia, it is important to know in what stage of dementia they are. I have a "mini mental test" that you can access on my website and download, or you can see in Appendix D. A family member can give the test to the loved one, get their score and determine what level of dementia they may or may not be experiencing.

It is important to discern exactly how many hours and how much help in a 24 hour period your senior needs help. Giving the mini mental test may help to determine how much and what kind of care they may need. Many people think that because In Home Health Services (IHHS) is a government county program, it's paid for by MediCal/Medicaid or Medicare, and this is also a myth. MediCal only pays for very low-income seniors, and a small number of hours for in-home care. Everyone else must pay privately for this care. IHHS does not pay for most seniors who need in-home health care services.

Another myth is that you must spend down your savings and assets in order to qualify for MediCal or Medicaid if you need to go into a SNF. This is absolutely not true! The government created medical entitlement programs especially to help people be able to leave their estates to their heirs, and not the state. Otherwise we would be creating ongoing impoverished generations.

I discuss more myths from my radio show and answer more questions about caregiving and finding care for your loved ones in my two e-books in Appendix E and on our website:

10 Frequently asked Questions for Caregivers: http://seniorcareofsacramento.com/10-frequently-asked-questions-for-caregivers

10 Things you need to "absolutely know", to find the best care for your aging parents:
http://seniorcareofsacramento.com/10-things-you-need-to-absolutely-know-to-find-the-best-care-for-your-aging-parents/

Chapter Four

Does Your Loved One Have Dementia?

Dementia care is more expensive as a rule even though in most cases for early and moderate stage dementia, people tend to be more high-functioning in their ability to do their own activities of daily living (ADL). These include assistance with bathing, dressing, grooming, eating and urine or bowel incontinence care. Many dementia patients can do their own ADL's with perhaps only minor help with incontinence, until they deteriorate in later stages of the disease.

Some people with dementia also suffer with behavioral issues related to the dementia. Cases with behavioral issues usually require an in-person assessment by a professional, and require caregivers who are trained to deal with dementia behaviors. Care is more expensive with this needed level of assistance.

It is crucial to know if someone has behavioral issues, diabetes or does not sleep at night. These 3 conditions require special attention and are more costly care needs. You will need to contact us to plumb these issues further; I do not go into the needs of caring for someone with these issues here because they require customized solutions for each individual's specific needs (and depends on their medications and doses, such as injection vs oral insulin etc.).

How do you get mom, dad or your spouse to accept help when they believe they don't need it?

Sometimes this is half the battle, not whether or not they can afford it! In situations like this seniors, caregivers, family members and loved ones need to ask themselves these questions:

- Are you the decision maker?
- Who do they rely on? You?
- Do they count on you for information?
- Do they listen to your feedback?
- Do you listen to their feedback?
- Is it important to educate them on their situation?
- Do you inform and educate them face to face?
- Do you listen to their personal needs?
- Do they listen to your personal needs, i.e., time, energy and money?
- How do you assist with or manage your loved one's fears?
- What are the ADL needs? Eating, bathing, medication, dressing, grooming?

- Is there resistance to change?
- Does your senior lack companionship?
- How do you manage the unknown?
- Do you convey information in a friendly and informative manner?
- Can technology be helpful? For example, with medication reminders, intercoms, phone check-ups, ID bracelets, life-alert pendants, security alarms on doors, GPS location tracking, movement sensors.
- Are there safety issues?
- What challenges are there? Are they physical, emotional, mental, financial challenges?
- What challenges are you dealing with? Time, money, energy, patience?
- What takes them out of their comfort zone? Strangers in their home, an inability to ask for help?
- What takes you out of your comfort zone? Is it incontinence care, discussions about money, no social life, no one to converse with?
- What are their fears about costs? And yours?
- Are they isolated?
- Are they lonely? Are you lonely?
- Are they getting enough stimulation, physically, emotionally, mentally, socially, spiritually?
- What are the alternatives?

- Is there a long-term care plan?

Asking and answering these questions for yourself and your loved one can aid in leading you to a conversation of resolution and compromise, if done with compassion and empathy. Of course, if both parties are not co-operating, or if dementia or cognizant impairment are part of the loved one's diagnosis, then it is necessary to bring in a professional to decipher the best plan of action and to support both parties in getting their needs met as harmoniously as possible.

Often it takes an objective, third party or authority figure to facilitate communication between family members. A senior may be more comfortable discussing their finances with a professional other than their children, for example. The older generation came from an era where respect for authority was and still is a time-honored tradition, so enlisting the aid and support of a financial advisor, medical doctor, or family lawyer can aid in developing co-operation in family situations of this nature. This can also aid in obtaining compliance with non-compliant seniors.

Note: THE IMPORTANCE OF A PROPER DIAGNOSIS IN ALL FORMS OF DEMENTIA

When someone exhibits the symptoms of dementia (memory loss, changes in language and math skills, disorientation) it is essential to have a thorough medical evaluation to determine the cause. Alzheimer's Disease is diagnosed through the process of ruling out other conditions which can cause similar symptoms of dementia.

Some of these conditions, unlike Alzheimer's, can be cured or reversed.

Please see our blog at www.SeniorCareofSacramento.com/ blog for the full information about the "Importance of a Proper Diagnosis" and examples of incorrect dementia diagnoses.

If you did not complete the mini mental test for your loved one with dementia in the previous chapter, do it now. (See Appendix D.) This test can help reveal things about your loved one's mental capacity that you may have been unaware. Sometimes when we are very close to someone or see them on a daily basis it is more difficult to be objective. You may want to consider having a professional assessment done by someone who has experience with dementia sufferers, especially if they have behavioral issues such as "acting out," "paranoia," "agitation," "insomnia," aggressive behavior or hostility, and lashing out physically, or wandering.

We here at Senior Care of Sacramento can help! Call us or go online and make an appointment with one of our consultants now to help you create a long-term care plan for yourself or your loved ones!

Web address: www.seniorcareofsacramento.com, email: seniorcareofsacramento@gmail.com; telephone: 916-877-6904.

Chapter Five

What is the Long Term Care Plan?

Step 1: The first and most important place to start for everyone including yourself is to complete an "Advanced Health Care Directive." (See Appendix F)

An "Advanced Healthcare Directive" simply lets the doctors, hospital and your family, know your wishes regarding your healthcare if you are unable to communicate your needs, wishes or desires for yourself, in the event of a medical emergency, i.e., stroke, heart attack.

Everyone should have one of these documents completed! If you have a trust, it should be included. Do read the form, making sure this still complies with your wishes, then let the person you appointed as your healthcare representative know you have appointed them, and what you expect from them. Your appointee should also have a copy of the directive. Without this document, a patient may be kept endlessly alive by machines, bankrupting the family or living a poor quality end of life.

I do not recommend giving a copy to your doctor or the hospital if they request it; this is because in this age of constant progressive technology, things are constantly changing. If your healthcare representative is clear on your wishes for the kind of quality of life or circumstances you wish to live, they can be better able to make the best choices for your healthcare needs, no matter how technology and life-saving methods in the healthcare industry change. Otherwise, hospitals and doctors are able to define the document in a way that may not be exactly what your wishes were.

I cannot stress enough the importance of having this Advanced Healthcare Directive (AHD) completed! **And a copy must be given to your representative or appointee**. This AHD can resolve issues in families and prevent problems down the road when no one knows what the loved one's wishes were, thus leaving everyone to guess. The AHD form only needs to be signed by an impartial witness (meaning no family members, caregivers, doctors etc.) and does not need to be notarized.

Step 2: The next step is **to complete a Power of Attorney (POA) form for your finances** (See Appendix F). A Power of Attorney (POA) form for finances allows you to appoint someone to be the authority for all legal or financial matters. I know this can be a frightening notion for some of you, but hopefully you have someone you trust enough to assign this important job. This would be someone who will pay your household bills for you if you are laid up in the hospital, even if it is temporary. This can be a friend, family member, or attorney. It is especially imperative to have a POA if you suspect you have Dementia or cognitive memory impairment.

Whether you have been diagnosed with Dementia (there are over 200 kinds of Dementia), Alzheimer disease or Mild Cognitive Impairment (MCI), it is crucial for you to appoint someone as your POA for health care and finances.

I have included POA forms in Appendix F. Remember to update these documents periodically! If you have a large estate and many investments you may wish to consult with an attorney, or if you already have a trust, then your POA has already been designated. Some trusts are made and forgotten. It is important to regularly consider who you want to designate and make sure these forms are updated.

Do you or your loved one have Dementia or cognitive Memory Impairment (MCI)?

Mild Cognitive Impairment is defined as deficits in memory that do not significantly impact daily functioning. The old term for this was usually referred to as "old age senility."

The diagnosis of MCI relies on the fact that the individual is able to perform all their usual activities of daily living successfully, without more assistance from others than they previously needed.

Memory problems may be minimal to mild, and hardly noticeable to the individual. Writing reminders and taking notes allow a person to compensate for memory difficulties. Unlike Alzheimer's Disease (AD) or Dementia where cognitive ability gradually declines, the memory deficits of MCI may remain stable for years.

However, some individuals with MCI develop cognitive deficits and functional impairment with AD or Dementia. Whether or not MCI is a disorder distinct from AD/Dementia or a very early phase of AD/Dementia is a topic of continuing investigation.

Note: Neither of the AHD or POA documents can be used unless the person who implemented them becomes incapacitated to the degree that they cannot perform such functions for themselves.

The forms are generally used in emergencies, or temporary situations such as after someone has had surgery or for end of life issues, with the exception of someone who has a diagnosis of Dementia or Alzheimer's. **In the case of AD or Dementia, these documents are essential to have completed as early as possible**.

If you wait until the person with these diseases is in the more advanced stages, you risk being deemed incompetent then and therefore without a voice. At that point, you will either have to hire an attorney or bear the lengthy time-consuming and costly expense of going to court to become the person's guardian or conservator.

It is because of the tremendous rise in the amount of AD and Dementia diagnoses in our country that I am encouraging everyone to have these documents completed early in order to avoid the misery and headache of having to go through a lengthy 9-12 month or more court process that is very time-consuming, and also involves doctor appointments and considerable expense.

In many cases, individuals who do not have these documents prepared in a timely fashion end up in a Skilled Nursing Facility (SNF) with no one advocating for them, at the mercy of strangers and a dysfunctional governmental system.

Don't let this happen to you and your loved ones!

If a senior is brought into a hospital emergency room (ER) due to a fall or dehydration, which are classic diagnoses, and they had no AHD or POA or advocate and if the hospital doctor diagnoses that individual with early stages of AD or Dementia, they could admit them to a SNF for their safety. These facilities must act on your behalf and follow protocols when there are no available AHDs or PDAs. At that point, the individual loses all independence and choices for his/her life.

Even if you are this person's next of kin, you could ultimately end up with no say in where your loved one is cared for, but still be sent a $9,000-$16,000 bill for a month of care at the SNF.

We never know what life is going to throw at us…so please have these documents completed early.

Tip: "Hospice" is care prescribed by a doctor's order when someone has been diagnosed with a terminal illness. It does not usually provide 24/7 non medical care, only part-time medical care. It is important to know that Hospice care is covered by MediCal and Medicare and that it is provided wherever the person needing it lives. It is not a place you go to get this level of care (although there are a rare few specialized Hospice facilities). Hospice comes to you wherever you are receiving your non medical care and daily activities of living care. i.e RCFE, ASL, SNF, Acute care hospital, or in your home.

Determining the Level of Care

Step 3: Review the financial assessment information you completed on our 3-page Health Assessment form to get an idea of your or your loved one's long-term and short-term care options. Use this form to help determine your loved one's care level, and monthly income. **If you have not completed the assessment form, do it now**.

On a separate paper, determine how many hours of care your loved one needs. If you are providing their care or part of their care for free, include how many hours you spend including medication management, ordering and picking up medications, paying bills, cleaning house, preparing meals, making doctor appointments, providing transportation to and from doctor's appointments plus labs, x-rays, physical therapy etc.

Step 4: The assessment forms help us to determine what "Level of Care" you or your loved one needs. It is important to know if you or your loved one is considered minimum, moderate or maximum care level.

Here Are the 3 Basic Definitions of the Levels of Care For Which Individuals Are Assessed:

1. **<u>Minimum Level of Care:</u>** This usually means that you need someone to cook and prepare your meals for you, provide transportation because you can no longer drive, clean the house, manage your medications and give them to you in the correct dose at the correct times, and order refills when necessary. It may also include supervision for safety, especially if you or your loved one has mild memory loss. They usually can

shower alone or only need someone to stand by for safety, to avoid slips and falls. Management of cash resources and bill paying is generally needed. It can, also, include minimal assistance with ADL's such as helping with buttons and zippers, putting shoes and socks on when dressing and undressing. This can also mean someone who needs assistance getting from a sitting position to a standing position but can then move around on their own, or with a walker, or cane.

2. **Moderate Level of Care:** This level of care includes all of the above care needs listed in number one minimum level of care but usually means the person needs more help with their ADL's. This means they need assistance with some or all of their ADL's like bathing, dressing, grooming and toileting. The person is most often incontinent with urine at this stage and needs assistance with toileting, and changing their undergarments (often padded Depends). They may need more assistance with dressing, or need some help to get dressed and undressed. Someone at this stage needs someone to help with minor hands-on care in the shower or may need help with washing their back or their hair. Someone at this stage may need someone to stand next to them when they

walk to prevent falls, especially if they are frail or weak, at risk of falling or have a history of falling. They may need to use a wheelchair due to pain issues but they can still stand and walk short distances with or without a walker.

3. **Maximum Level of Care:** This level of care includes all of the care needed in number two moderate level of care but this also means that the person is completely dependent on someone else for all or almost all their care needs. This may mean they cannot ambulate without one or two people helping them to get to their feet or to transfer to a wheelchair. Or they may not be able to lift their own weight at all and their caregiver or caregivers may have to lift them, especially if they are *dead weight* due to paralysis, stroke, general malaise or weakness. This is the most expensive type of care and why it is so important to exercise. Keep moving, use your muscles and stay in as good a shape physically as possible. This type of care can limit your choices for RCFE as only a handful do this type of heavy (lifting) care. It can be the defining of your placement for care in an RCFE versus a skilled nursing hospital. Not only is this kind of placement expensive and out of most people's budget, there are few RCFE's willing to do

this kind of heavy lifting. They just do not have the staffing to do it.

(There are four industries competing for our caregiver labor force: acute care hospitals, skilled nursing hospitals, assisted living facilities/board and care homes and in-home healthcare agencies. Yet, there is a shortage of caregivers; partially due to poor pay and no benefits, but mainly because of a shrinking age appropriate labor force.)

Now that you have a better idea of what level of care you or your loved one requires we can move on to figuring out how much it is going to cost for that care. And, of course, you must decide if you or your senior can afford that care. And if not, begin to look at resources to determine eligibility to qualify for financial help for future care so you can plan ahead.

Step Five: Determining the budget costs for caregiving.

See the worksheet in Appendix C or on our website here: http://seniorcareofsacramento.com/comparison-worksheet-for-assisted-living-board-and-care

I will be using the current care costs from California (which are pretty close to the National median figures) to help you get a good idea what it is going to cost you for you or your loved one's care.

We will start with in-home care. You can figure at today's prices it is going to cost you $25 an hour if you need minimum or moderate level of care for a licensed, bonded caregiver from an In Home Health Service or Agency who provide screened fingerprinted caregivers. This is assuming you are using a reputable licensed In Home Care Service. All In Home Care Services in California are now required to be licensed by the State of California; **always ask for their license number to know that you are working with a licensed service**. I don't believe all the states have implemented this regulation so it is important that you use a referral service such as **Senior Care of Sacramento** to get referrals to reputable In Home Care Services, especially if your state is not yet regulating In Home Care Service Agencies.

Be aware not all In Home Care Services are comparable. There are three types of In Home Care Services (IHCS).

First, there are some IHCS that are paid for by your health insurances. But these IHCS provide strictly registered nurses (RN's) or licensed vocational nurses (LVN's), with a doctor's order, and are temporary and limited to several hours a week. These agencies only send out RN's and LVN's, Physical Therapists (PT), and Occupational Therapists (OT) for follow up care when a patient has been discharged from an acute care hospital or a SNF, but not usually for more than six weeks. They are only doing follow-up rehab treatments and tests to help you recover from whatever sent you to the hospital. These agencies do not provide for non-medical caregiving needs such as the levels of care I discussed previously. Those are the activities of daily living (ADLs) of bathing, dressing, grooming, feeding, and incontinence care.

In California, in-home care services are not to be confused with In Home Health Services (IHHS), a federal program that is provided by the County for low-income individuals on MediCal/Medicaid

IHCS agencies only provide licensed medical care follow up from RNs, LVNs, PT and OTs. As a rule, these services are only short term oversight medical professionals who give you 1-3 hours a week of supervision for your follow-up to your hospital stay and who report your progress back to your doctor. Your doctor can order IHCS if you need them regardless of whether or not you were hospitalized as well, but they only do this occasionally for specific issues. They can be very helpful and usually have a social worker on staff who can refer you to local IHCS agencies. We also provide this referral service at Senior Care of Sacramento, for **non-medical care** and the second type of IHCS available to provide caregivers who can assist in the home with the usual ADL's required.

This type of IHCS, a non-medical IHCS, is not covered by healthcare insurance companies; they are all private pay. Many people are confused and misinformed thinking that IHCS are paid by Medi Cal/Medicaid or Medicare because of the confusion between the two types of IHCS **medical** and **non-medical**. Hopefully, you understand the difference now.

There is a county run in-home care service called In Home Health Service (IHHS) that is provided for very low-income individuals who qualify for Medi Cal/Medicaid, and Medicare but it is very minimal and underfunded. To qualify for these services, basically your only income is usually Social Security of $1,500 a month or less, and you own no investments or assets of more than $2,000 (usually a car). The most caregiver help you can get is 40 hours every 2 weeks and they only pay $10 an hour to a caregiver of your choice, who has completed the county orientation program and fingerprinting process (even if the caregiver is a family member). Few people qualify for the maximum number of hours, twenty hours a week. It generally takes 30-90 days to establish and qualify for these caregiving services. Family members can be the paid caregiver for the senior. The senior must need assistance with a minimum of 2 to 3 ADL's daily to qualify for these services, and may need 24 hour supervision for safety if they have dementia, but even if they are deemed to need 24 hour supervision and qualify, you most likely will not receive 24 Hour paid caregiver hours. The funding is just not available

You can purchase "Long Term Care Insurance" (LTCI) separately that will pay for non-medical IHCS but the premiums are out of reach for most middle income and lower income Americans. Many of the LTCI companies are unscrupulous and have bad reputations, so you must choose wisely and do your due diligence research and homework when choosing the insurance company. Better yet, use a reputable insurance agent to help you choose a good one.

There is one last type of IHCS and these are disappearing with the new state regulations for IHCS. But a few are still out there. These IHCS are usually companies with names like "Companion Care" and are non-medical services and do not provide ADL's services. Basically, they only provide "Companion Care;" they will keep you or your loved one company. They are also strictly private pay; no insurance pays for this service, not even LTCI companies. Some of them will take you out to eat in a restaurant or to a movie, or just to go for a ride, and some of them won't. They each offer different types of "visiting" services and many people use them as a type of glorified babysitting service for their loved ones, in order to allow them to run errands. They are often available for an hour, as a rule. These companion care services will not help you or your loved one with ambulating, housework, cooking, dressing, or toileting, so keep this in mind.

The IHCS that most people will need to hire is the non-medical private pay caregivers who can provide all the care of daily activities of living, bathing, dressing, grooming, toileting and ambulating in addition to light house cleaning, cooking, laundry, and transportation to doctors, outings and medication management.

Most people who fall into the Level I and Level II of Care should expect to pay at least $25 per hour for all these non-medical services. For people falling into Level III Care you can expect to pay $25 and up to $40 per hour if you are considered heavy care or total care and or require lifting.

At the point when someone is at a Level III Care, it is usually cost prohibitive to stay at home. It will be more affordable and cost effective to be in assisted living or skilled nursing, depending on their financial resources.

Another thing to take into consideration is that most IHCS non-medical companies want you to purchase a minimum of 3-4 hours per visit in order for them to provide you a caregiver. There are a very few who occasionally will do a split shift of 2 hours in the morning and 2 hours at night to help someone get up in the morning and have breakfast and then come back and help someone have dinner and get back to bed. They are few and far between and will only do this depending on their staffing abilities.

When you are considering costs for IHCS you can typically calculate, based on the level of care you or your loved one needs, how many hours a week/month is needed. If you have figured out how many hours of caregiving services you will need you can calculate the cost using this sampling of what most people end up paying out-of-pocket for caregiving:

Hours per day	Visits per week	Hours per week	Hourly rate	Per week	Per month
4	2	8	$25	$200	$800
4	3	12	$25	$300	$1200
6	3	18	$25	$450	$1800
8	4	32	$25	$800	$3200
8	5	40	$25	$1000	$4000
8	7	56	$25	$1400	$5600
10	7	70	$25	$1750	$7000

(Prices are for California but the rest of the US does not vary much from these figures.)

You can see how quickly caregiving costs add up and how expensive it can be. At the point you are paying $3,200 a month for only 32 hours a week of care most likely that is not enough caregiving hours, and that means you are not getting the care you need for the 3 days a week you cannot afford. Or if you can afford someone to come in 7 days a week at only 8 hours a day and you're paying $5,600, then it is time to consider moving to a RCFE because it will be much more cost effective and you will get 24 hours a day, 7 days a week care for the same price you are paying to stay at home, at only 8 hours a day. Plus, you will be saving the monthly cost and maintenance of your household expenses that you are paying on top of your care.

See the comparison sheet Appendix C to do the calculation comparisons to see how much money you can save or put toward your future caregiving needs in an assisted living RCFE or board and care.

Take into consideration that, currently, the average monthly cost for an RCFE for someone at a Level I Care is $3,500 in California. You can quickly see how moving to an RCFE or Board and Care is much more cost-effective than staying at home and receiving much less caregiving for the same amount of money. Most middle income Americans find it is better to consider moving to an RCFE or Board and Care at this point, unless they have other resources available to them, such as family caregivers or financial resources they can access.

This leads us to our next chapter in which we will help you find money to pay for your caregiving needs now or in the future. Now that you have a pretty good idea of what care costs are and what kind of budget you will need to pay for your care needs, let's see if you need some help to pay for those caregiving costs.

Chapter Six

Best Options and Referral Resources Available to Help Pay for Caregiving Needs

Let's determine if you're eligible for any of the following resources.

First, there are many resources available for seniors and you will find a list in the Appendix titled More Resources and Links. Unfortunately, too many of these resources are so bogged down in bureaucracy they are dysfunctional or useless. The good news is that there are six excellent resources that are well worth your time and energy to pursue, and can make a big difference in the quality of care you receive. These are the resources where I have placed people and recommend to my clients on a regular basis. I have chosen them because I believe they can help make the best positive difference for many seniors.

The most useful resources that can help seniors in saving their assets for their children and grandchildren and helping them to pay for their caregiving needs are:

1) Asset protection

2) Veteran Aid and Attendance Benefits

3) MediCal or Medicaid/Medicare

4) Long Term Care Insurance

5) Assisted Living Waiver Programs

6) Tax deduction for caregiving.

More specific definitions of each of these benefits will be explained in Chapter 7. First, I want to give you some practical information about these programs to save you time, energy and money. MediCal/Medicaid and the Assisted Living Waiver Program (ALW) are helpful mainly for low-income and sometimes low-to-middle income American seniors. Asset protection and the Veteran Aid and Attendance Benefits are more for upper middle to upper-income Americans. Although, VA Aid and Attendance is also available to lower income veterans as well. Tax deduction is for all taxpayers. Many people are on the borderline when it comes to their income as to which class tax bracket they fit into, so sometimes these resources can cross over class income levels. This is why it is crucial to get consultations with a geriatric care manager to guide you through the process or eligibility requirements.

Geriatric Care Management Pays For Itself

The cost of hiring a geriatric care manager is a fraction of the savings they produce. Geriatric care management results in better health and financial outcomes, easily paying for itself over a period of a few years or less. Geriatric care management also provides more cash in the bank because the senior's family members will not be absent from work as much and are less likely to have to leave the workforce to care for the parent.

Care managers reduce caregiver stress and act as an objective third party mediator, resolving family conflicts and minimizing family disputes related to long term care. When a senior's life is better, the family life is better too.

A geriatric care manager plans and coordinates the care and safety of the elderly to improve their quality of life and to maintain their independence. They have extensive knowledge about the availability, quality, and costs of elder care services and communities in their city or region. Care managers are experts at sorting through the array of challenging decisions facing an aging senior and their family and can help to identify the best solutions. The family is usually experiencing this for the first time, whereas the care manager has been there many times.

A geriatric care manager uses training and experience with issues related to aging and elder care including social work, gerontology, nursing, nutrition, and psychology, in order to be the point person and advocate for a senior, often with a focus on maintaining the senior's independence for as long as possible. Geriatric care managers often help manage chronic needs for those suffering from Alzheimer's disease or other dementia.

A geriatric care manager can act as a liaison on all matters concerning the senior for families that provide long-distance care. The care manager can keep track of all documents and instructions for a long distance senior to ensure that the senior's treatment is consistent, whether they are living at home, in an assisted living setting, board and care, or a nursing home. The care manager can save the family money with crisis management so that out-of-town family members don't spend top dollar for emergency travel because of an unexpected hospitalization or other crisis, and acts as a liaison to the family at a distance, updating them through emails, phone calls, or a mobile app.

Geriatric care managers help individuals, caregivers, and families adjust and cope with the challenges of aging by doing any number of the following:

- Audit the home for fall risks and provide a referral to a contractor for safety retrofitting if necessary.
- Help make arrangements to purchase or rent medical equipment for lifting, moving, and ease of use of the bathroom facilities.

- Screen, arrange, monitor, and support in-home help and/or caregivers.
- Visit the senior on a routine basis to make sure they are safe, and ensure the senior is eating and that there's food in the refrigerator and cupboards.
- Make sure prescriptions are refilled and watch for medication hazards such as not taking medication on time or taking the wrong dosage.
- Monitor the senior's finances and bill paying.
- Identify unnecessary services such as excess medical testing or overlapping caregiver shifts.
- Monitor against fraud or elder abuse.
- Make medical appointments and assure the senior gets to them, perhaps personally providing transportation to appointments, and then making sure doctors' orders are understood and followed.
- Advise on Medicare and Medicaid coverage and Veterans Administration benefits, uncover unused benefits, and provide a referral to a specialist to help with eligibility of complex benefits and asset protection strategies and tactics including asset transfers, gifting, and trust set up.
- Provide a referral to an elder law attorney who will prepare powers of attorney and a living will.
- Recommend a reverse mortgage specialist.

- Provide appropriate placement into an appropriate assisted living or nursing community so that the senior does not have to be moved again or repeatedly.

- Assist with moving their clients to or from a retirement complex, assisted living facility, rehabilitation facility, or nursing home.

- Monitor the care of a senior in assisted living or a nursing home.

Hiring a geriatric care manager for either a one-time assessment with a written plan or for ongoing support will lower expenses in the long run by helping you plan ahead and avoid hasty decisions that end up being avoidable and expensive. Your geriatric care manager can arrange and manage the process of building a "circle of care" in which family members, friends, and community members help with caregiving duties such as driving, grocery shopping, and simply spending time with your loved one.

To determine if you are eligible for asset protection, you obviously need to own some assets. Any assets that you own that you want your children or grandchildren, relatives, etc. to inherit can be willed, deeded, or assigned through traditional means of a trust or last will and testament. For our purposes here, we are concerned about preserving your assets and preventing them from being usurped by caregiving, skilled nursing hospital and medical costs. Caregiving and end of life care is very expensive and can quickly evaporate any savings or assets a senior has, especially when accruing a $300 a day skilled nursing (SNF) bill. And as we have already discussed, long term care, assisted living, skilled nursing care, and in-home care is not covered by Health Insurance such as Blue Cross, Blue Shield, Kaiser, or any of the other Health Plans out there. Neither does MediCal, Medicaid or MediCare (unless your only income is Social Security and you basically have no assets, then MediCal or Medicaid will take all of your Social Security income (except about $37) to pay the rest of your SNF bill). But MediCal or Medicaid will generally not pay.

So, to be clear, **if you want your insurance to pay for your long term care, you must purchase Long Term Care Insurance (LTCI)**. Long Term Care Insurance is also very expensive, approximately $500 a month for a decent policy in today's economy. LTC insurance is an excellent option if you can afford it. I highly recommend it if you can afford it. It is a great solution for LTC. But make sure it is a reputable company; do your homework on this or get advice from an expert. Unfortunately, the LTC Insurance industry has been plagued with unethical companies. I discuss LTC Insurance in more detail in the next chapter. Unfortunately, most people I see do not have it, can't afford it, or didn't purchase it when it was affordable.

So what to do to save your assets so your children can inherit? The State fortunately does have a long term benefit plan for seniors. It is available through MediCal or Medicaid but in order to qualify for it you will need someone who is a specialist who knows how to maneuver through the MediCal or Medicaid system to get the LTC benefit. There are a very few experts who know how to do the paperwork and get the MediCal or Medicaid benefit applications qualified and accepted by MediCal or Medicaid Departments. Even when low-income (SSI only) applicants need to apply for LTC MediCal or Medicaid, it is not easy to get the application approved either. These low-income applications are accepted more than those with assets. Both types of recipients must complete the applications perfectly...crossing every "T" and dotting every "i," or the applications are regularly rejected and you have to start all over again, waiting another 3 to 12 months for the application to be reprocessed. Most MediCal applications in California are taking 3 to 12 months to be processed when consumers apply for SNF/LTC benefits. The exception is if the senior is already in a SNF and their 30-120 day Medicare paid benefit has expired. Then the SNF staff will apply for the patient so the hospital can get paid. They are sometimes able to get the MediCal or Medicaid applications processed sooner than the consumers applying before they have been admitted to SNF.

Experts who charge to do the MediCal or Medicaid applications for recipients who are not low income charge on average $3,500 and up, depending on the amount of assets they need to help protect. If your assets are in an **irrevocable trust** then they may not be able to help you. It is important to use an elder law attorney who knows what kind of trust to set up for you so you do not get disqualified from other benefit programs that may otherwise be available to you.

Generally, you will need to use more than one financial expert to set up your asset protection. I recommend one asset protection expert who works with an attorney (but you can also use your own attorney, if you prefer) and my guy knows all the eligibility requirements for MediCal, Medicare and the Veterans Benefits (which I will discuss next). Many attorneys are not aware of the MediCal, Medicare, and Veteran Benefits eligibility requirements we are discussing which is why some seniors end up with trusts that cannot be converted to allow the senior to qualify for these benefits and resources.

I do not claim to be a financial advisor but I do know the eligibility requirements that my clients need to qualify for the MediCal/Medicaid, and Veterans Aid and Attendance Benefits. I can help someone get benefits using an expert to help them through the process once I have determined if they qualify for these healthcare benefits. The health care benefits I am talking about are for caregiving needs and costs.

I do not advise trying to do MediCal or Veteran Aid and Attendance Benefits applications yourself as they are routinely rejected. And then you have to start over or appeal; this can make the process take even longer. Veterans Aid and Attendance Benefits are currently taking 30-90 days to be processed and applicants for spouses of the Veterans Aid and Attendance Benefits are taking 6-9 months to be processed in California. So you can see why rejected applications can create worse delays. The good thing about the Veterans Aid and Attendance Benefits is that they are retroactive so the benefit will be reimbursed if you qualify from the date you submitted your application. But you have to know to ask for the retroactive amount in your application. Be aware that it is illegal for anyone to charge you for helping you to complete a Veterans Aid and attendance application.

MediCal applications are retroactive for only 90 days as a rule. This is only for low-income SSI recipients, not necessarily if you are applying and have not yet qualified for asset protection. If your only asset is the home you live in and it is not paid off you may not have enough of an asset to worry about protecting through this MediCal benefit. Although your home is automatically protected up to a certain amount for both you and your spouse, if you have a home, for example, that is paid off and worth $500,000 or more then you will want to protect it from the state putting a lien on it to pay your SNF Medical bill.

The Veteran Aid and Attendance Benefit for Veterans and the Veteran Aid and Attendance Benefits for Spouses can be a lifesaver for senior veterans over 60 to help pay for their care and/or their spouses care. The maximum benefit a married veteran can qualify for currently is around $2,000 a month for both himself and his spouse. A veteran can qualify for up to almost $1,900 a month just for himself and a veteran's surviving spouse can receive up to $1,200 a month for caregiving needs. These monies can be used to help pay for in-home caregivers or Assisted Living RCFE Care, but not for SNF care. This can mean the difference for a senior veteran being able to stay at home with a better quality of care than he might not otherwise receive.

It is not widely published but much of the millions of dollars Governor Schwarzenegger put aside for the benefit for veterans is just waiting to be used for veterans. Please let your veteran know about it. Having $2,000 more a month can be a life changer for a veteran. Veterans can be receiving their regular disability pension from the service and still qualify for this additional benefit after the age of 60 to help pay for their care, if they are not already receiving a 100% disability pension. If they already receive the maximum of 100% permanent disability pension (currently about $4,000 a month) then the $1,900 Aid and Attendance Benefit would be deducted from their maximum permanent pension and they would not qualify for more monies. But any Veteran not receiving 100% maximum permanent disability pension could qualify for up to the $1,900 maximum Aid and Attendance Benefits after age 60 to help pay for their care.

Some people know that the VA will pay a monthly benefit to any active-duty veteran or their spouse who needs care. Most people don't know about another extremely valuable Veteran Administration Aid and Attendance Benefit that has been in place for over 60 years; any veteran who has served even one day during a period of foreign war can apply for Aid and Attendance Special Pension to pay for Senior Services. No history of foreign deployment whatsoever is required to qualify.

Only 9% of people eligible for this enormously valuable benefit know about it, and even less apply for it and use it.

Any vet who has difficulties with two or more activities of daily living, such as bathing, dressing, eating, medication, and money management, and also any difficulty with financial planning, is likely to be eligible. The senior's disability or care needs can be entirely non-service-related.

A veteran or his or her survivor is allowed to pay friends or family members to help them, whether or not the caregivers are licensed professionals or an employee of a licensed in-home care agency.

Aid and Attendance is means tested; based on an accounting of assets and income. The vet or survivor will get the full benefit when 100% of income is being paid out in care and services. Meeting or exceeding an asset maximum can disqualify the senior from getting the benefit. But this is where our asset protection expert can come in, because it depends on how you are holding your assets.

For more details on eligibility, qualifications, and how the asset protection and Veterans Aid and Attendance Benefits work, please listen to the audio file interviews I did with experts Dale Drury and Gabe Lenhart, ESQ, at my website at http://seniorcareofsacramento.com.

Next, I want to talk about MediCal or Medicaid (one and the same thing) and IHHS. Many times, seniors may be paying exorbitant fees for medications and co-pays for doctor visits, labs, x-rays, etc. and not realize it. I have consulted with many seniors who had a very poor health insurance plan OR they had the same plan since they retired from their employer. Often it was considered the best health insurance available at that time and so they never bothered to look into updating it or checking to see if perhaps there were better policies available now. They assumed they were locked into these employer health plans.

It is always a good idea to review your policies annually, especially in our current healthcare policy variances. I have been able to get seniors a $300 to $500 per month reduction from their health insurance premiums though they are still receiving the exact same healthcare benefits and coverage…just by having them change healthcare policies. This allowed many of my clients to be able to afford some in-home care or move to an ASL/RCFE that previously was out of their budget. A few hundred dollars a month can make a big difference when it comes to being able to stay at home or move to an ASL/RCFE.

Please take the time to meet with an insurance agent who represents many healthcare insurance companies, not just one, and let them help you find the best healthcare policy for your particular medical needs and expenses. They are very diverse. Many seniors don't realize they can have private health insurance and also qualify for MediCal or Medicaid. Many people can qualify for both. MediCal or Medicaid and Medicare can help pay for your private health insurance premiums, co-pays, medications, medical equipment such as wheelchairs, walkers, and commodes. If you are paying for an in-home caregiver for example, you probably need any and all monies available to you for your caregiver costs. In my experience, many seniors are having caregivers come in and help them based on what they can afford instead of the amount of help and care they need, usually because they cannot afford the actual amount of caregiving hours they really need. One way to offset this imbalance is to apply for Medi Cal/Medicaid to cover the additional costs you may be paying for premiums, medications, co-pays, medical equipment, etc., so that you can use that money towards your caregiving needs and costs instead.

The problem, as I stated before, is that the MediCal/Medicaid system is so cumbersome and difficult to maneuver that you really need to hire an expert to submit your application for you. There are quite a few more experts doing this now. It is best to ask around and get recommendations from people you know. I have several people I recommend to do this for my clients.

You can find an interview on this subject with Carol Costa Smith from The Light for Seniors in a free download on our website at www.SeniorCareofSacramento.com.

Carol is worth her weight in gold. I enlisted Carol to apply for MediCal for my mother at the same time I was applying for the Veterans Aid and Attendance (VA) Benefits for her. It took 3 different experts to help my mom get the funds and services she needed to get the quality care she deserved after devoting over 45 years to the nursing profession. As one of these experts who works in the healthcare industry and knows what is required to get applications through our healthcare system to acquire needed care services for seniors, I can tell you not enough seniors have someone like me or Carol to help them and are being neglected. 95% of caregivers are daughters and daughters-in-law. So I always tell women to be nice to their daughters-in-law--they could end up needing their care.

These statistics are staggering and too many women must quit their jobs or cut back to part-time to care for a loved one, right at a time in life when they need to be saving for their own retirement and aging care. This is exactly why the government created the Medical Entitlement Programs like my mother receives to help pay for her care so I and my sister could keep working or at least be paid something while caring for our mother. Otherwise who will be paying for our care and the next generation? The asset protection program was put in place so that families could leave their fortune or estates to their heirs and to help preserve the family unit. So don't let anyone tell you that MediCal or Medicaid for seniors is welfare or spending down your assets is necessary to get MediCal or Medicaid. This is poor advice, so seek out a financial expert.

There is another program that not many people have heard of called the "Assisted Living Waiver Program" or ALWP (now called ALW). I mentioned earlier that I sponsored this program into becoming law in California. This program was MediCal reform law which allows seniors who have low-income and little to no assets move to an RCFE, using their Social Security income, and the state and federal government will supplement the cost of the RCFE that their SSI does not cover. There are currently many restrictions, specific criteria, and limitations on this program. It is currently limited to a few counties in California and only available to several thousand residents at a certain level of care. The intent is for the ALW to be opened up statewide and that all low-income seniors will have a choice to stay at home or go to an RCFE, instead of a SNF. Yet, California will pay $6-$16,000 a month for someone to be in a SNF vs. an RCFE for $2,000-$5,000 a month. As I have said previously, our healthcare system is dysfunctional.

I am discussing this government program to make you aware of it in the event you may be one of the lucky ones able to apply and qualify for those benefits, and in the hope that California and other States will soon open it up to everyone who qualifies, not just a select few.

If you are low-income and would like to see if you qualify for this ALW to get In Home Caregiver help or funds to move to an RCFE, go to www.ALWP.org and apply. There is usually a waiting list to get on the program and it can take up to a year unless you are in a SNF and waiting for an RCFE, then I understand the wait is considerably shorter. It is best to check the program's website to see the current status of which counties are being served and which counties are being added as they are always adding more counties and making adjustments to the program.

Here is more information on the Assisted Living Waiver Program: Assisted Living Waiver (ALW)
http://www.dhcs.ca.gov/SERVICES/LTC/Pages/ALWP.aspx

The ALW pilot program was determined to be successful during the first three years in a limited trial in three counties. In March 2009, the Centers for Medicare and Medicaid Services approved a waiver renewal for an additional five years and expansion of the program into additional counties. A five-year waiver renewal was effective March 1, 2014.The ALW is currently enrolling beneficiaries residing in skilled nursing facilities and in the community into licensed Residential Care Facilities (RCFEs) in Alameda, Contra Costa, Fresno, Kern, Los Angeles, Orange, Riverside, Sacramento, San Bernardino, San Diego, San Joaquin, San Mateo, Santa Clara, and Sonoma counties.

Periodically the ALW will put a hold or freeze on enrollments throughout the year until they can catch up with the demand. So keep checking back if this is the case or plan ahead and apply early.

You may reach them directly:

ALW
Long-Term Care Division
1501 Capitol Avenue, MS 4503
PO Box 997419
Sacramento, CA 95899-7419
Phone: 916-552-9105

Centers for Medicare and Medicaid, Medicaid Waivers, CA
Assisted Living
Bernie Finneran, Health Program Manager I
Assisted Living Waiver
Long-Term Care Division
Department of Health Care Services
1501 Capitol Avenue, MS 4502
P.O. Box 997419
Sacramento, CA 95899-7419
(916) 552-9322
Email to: Bernard.Finneran@dhcs.ca.gov

California Community Transitions - A New Program for Medi-Cal beneficiaries living in Skilled Nursing Facilities

Elder Options is now partnering with the Department of Health Care Services as a Lead Organization in a new demonstration project called California Community Transitions (CCT). This exciting program offers some new choices for people living in a Skilled Nursing Facility (SNF) who are on Medi-Cal, and want to explore the possibilities of moving back to the community.

The CCT program is a "Money Follows the Person" rebalancing demonstration funded by the Centers for Medicare and Medicaid Services. The program is designed to save government money by assisting people to return to their homes and communities with assistance from the state. Money that would have been spent keeping the person in a hospital can be spent assisting that person to stay at home with available services, usually for a lot less.

The CCT program is designed to assist those people who have lived continuously in a SNF for at least 6 months, who have been on Medi-cal for at least 30 days, and who want to transition back into their community, but don't have the resources to do so. The CCT program in my estimation is an extension of the ALW program (which already provided the same service that CCT is now providing.) Basically the only difference is that CCT is giving priority to SNF residents over community consumers.

The CCT program identifies eligible participants and assists them in transitioning out of nursing care and back into a community setting; either at home with family, in an apartment, or living with 2-3 others in similar situations. The program identifies supports and services available in the community, arranges training for family caregivers, makes modifications to homes and vehicles, and just about anything else someone would need to make the transition. A professional care manager works closely with the participant and their family, arranges needed services, then assists the participant throughout the process and for a year after the transition is made. The program is voluntary, saves money and helps people return to the community. Call Elder Options at 530-626-6939 for more information.

The last little tip I want to give you before we move on to more money matters has to do with taxes. Here is some tax advice on how you can claim medical expenses as a tax deduction for assisted living care.

Tip: You can get a tax deduction for being a caregiver or even just managing a family member's care. Ask your tax accountant to look it up and that you want your $1,000 tax write off for managing your mom's or dad's medications all year or for moving them from their home to an RCFE, or whatever care or care management services you provided them! See this article below.

Medical Expense Deductions for Assisted Living Costs

A senior usually has to be "chronically and permanently" ill to take a deduction for assisted living costs, but not always. Costs for a stay of a few months in an assisted living facility, such as a stay necessitated for recovery from a hospital operation, may be tax deductible. There are IRS restrictions and thresholds in place. Residents who are not chronically ill may still deduct the portion of their expenses that are attributable to medical care, including processing and entrance fees.

If you have burdensome bills or debt due to a temporary stay at an assisted living facility of, say, a few months, consult with a tax professional to see if you may be able to mitigate some of the burden with tax deductions even though you did not exactly meet the exact criteria for being "chronically ill."

Because the law can be unclear, it is essential to consult with an accountant or tax attorney before taking all but the most clear cut medical deductions for assisted living costs. With that in mind, here are some guidelines for deducting medical expenses associated with residency at an assisted living home or community.

Costs for living in a "residential care community" or "assisted living board & care home" vary vastly, from as little as $1500 per month, to the more typical $3,500 to $4,500 per month, all the way up to $5,000 to $6,000 per month for dementia care. Few people have long-term care insurance to pay for residential care home costs should the need arise. Medicare will not pay for custodial care or assisted living costs. And most people will not qualify for Medicaid to pay medical expenses at an assisted living community. Most Americans try to mitigate the cost of assisted living expenses through tax deductions.

In most cases, qualification for deductions are allowed only for medical or assisted activities of daily living care services provided according to a plan of care prescribed by a doctor, nurse, or licensed social worker. Assisted living expenses are tax deductible as medical expenses when the primary reason for the senior's presence at an assisted living community or board & care home is to receive care. The doctor, nurse, or social worker must certify in a prepared plan that the resident either:

- Cannot perform at least two activities of daily living, such as eating, toileting, transferring, bathing, dressing, or continence;
- Or requires supervision due to a cognitive impairment or dementia.

If the resident is chronically ill and in the facility primarily for medical care, and the care is being performed according to a certified care plan, then the room and board may be considered part of the medical care and all costs may be deductible, just as they would be in a hospital. The care facility may indicate to you that you likely qualify for a tax deduction, but, again, you must consult with a tax professional to know for sure.

A son or daughter can deduct the medical care expenses for a parent from their own taxes if they pay, in a given tax year, more than 50% of the parent's support costs. The IRS allows a deduction from income tax for medical care of the taxpayer, the taxpayer's spouse, or a dependent. Deductions may be taken on expenses paid during the taxable year that were not compensated for by insurance or otherwise when the total uncompensated expenses exceed 7.5% of adjusted gross income.

IRS rules specify that if an individual is in a "home for the aged" for personal or family reasons, and not because he or she requires medical attention, meals and lodging at the home are not deductible as the cost of medical care. But even residents who are not chronically ill may still deduct the portion of their expenses that are attributable to medical care, including processing and entrance fees. And when the provision of medical care is the central reason for the person's presence at a care home or assisted living community, and meals and lodging are furnished as necessary for provision of care, the entire cost of medical care and lodging and meals qualifies as a tax deductible expense for medical care.

Lodging, food, and other costs incurred for the spouse of a resident who moves into assisted living facility for the primary purpose of residing with the spouse needing care are not deductible.

Chapter Seven

Additional Ways to Pay for Long Term Care

Paying for Seniors' Needs

In this chapter we will discuss how to fund senior care with additional government programs, insurance, and loans. We will go far beyond the obvious ways one might fund short term financial needs, such as using a credit card, liquidating luxury assets like diamond jewelry, gold, or a high-end watch to cash or a cash loan, selling a car or boat. And we will take a deep dive into ways to fund long-term in-home or residential care needs. When it comes to your home, I always advocate as a last resort to fund your LTC through its sale. We also advocate creating asset protection first to preserve your equity and assets, and to avail yourself of the previous government programs I discussed in Chapter 6, before you have to dip into your home, or lose it.

Free Unclaimed Money

Scott Parkin, a National Council On Aging (NCOA) vice president, in interview with the U.S. News and World Report said "There are lots of programs out there to make ends meet, but it's rare that more than half the people who qualify actually use them."

Benefits Aggregation Websites

The National Council on Aging (NCOA) benefit website www.BenefitsCheckUp.org is America's most used benefits directory and search engine. It is responsible for helping more U.S. citizens find benefits programs for which they qualify than any other single website. BenefitsCheckUp.org will point you to one or more of the 2,000+ federal, state, and local benefits programs that help pay for health care, prescription drugs, food, housing, foreclosure prevention assistance, and long-term care planning. Start by answering a series of questions to zero in on benefits that could help cover or lessen the costs for you, your loved one, or your friend.

Eldercare Locator at Eldercare.gov is a public service of the U. S. Administration for Community Living and is administered by the National Association of Area Agencies on Aging. Its mission is to help older adults and caregivers identify resources including transportation, home and community-based services, adult day programs, elder abuse prevention, home repair and modification, legal assistance, and volunteer groups. The Locator's National Call Center, toll-free 800-677-1116, is open Monday through Friday from 9am to 8pm.

If you are looking for private In Home Care or a residential care facility for the elderly RCFE or ASL then it is best to call an agency such as SCOS because Elder Care

Locator will only refer you to county low income In Home Care Agencies not private pay agencies and they will refer you to the Department of Health for RCFE's not a customized list for your loved one.

Insurance

Long-Term Care Insurance

Though we will cover a lot here, your best source for learning all about LTC Insurance is The American Association of Long-Term Care Insurance's YouTube Channel.

Still have questions or need a list of vetted LTC insurance agents for your location? You can call The American Association of Long-Term Care Insurance at 818-597-3227. They are in California with Pacific Time office hours.

Other Long-Term Care Resources:

National Care Planning Council, Centerville, Utah, 801-298-8676

National Clearinghouse for Long Term Care Information, Administration on Aging, LongTermCare.gov, Washington DC, Phone: 202-619-0724

Long-term care insurance can be used to fund a spectrum of long term senior care needs; everything from adult day care, in-home non-medical care, in-home and residential skilled nursing, assisted living community rent and other expenses, and nursing home care. Long-term care insurance can also cover costs that Medicare, Medicaid, and primary private health insurance fail to cover. Premiums are either non-taxed or tax-deductible.

What Might a Financial Liquidity Crisis Caused by Long-Term Care Costs Look Like?

First consider that Medicare, Medicaid and other traditional health insurance plans may not cover long-term care. Medicare usually won't pay for long-term in-home care or skilled nursing facility care at all. Then consider that the cost of long-term care can exceed a middle class senior's ability to pay in a frighteningly short span of time. The cost of a licensed practical nurse provided by a professional home care agency is about $38 per hour, and even more in states like California and New York, and in any metro area with a hot economy, like the San Francisco Bay Region and the Washington DC Capital Region. A home health aide provided by an agency cost $25 per hour and more. Nursing home stays can cost upwards of $75,000 per year.

U.S. median annual costs for LTC (half cost less and half more):

- Nursing home, private room $80,000
- Semi-private room, $72,000

- Assisted living community, 1-bedroom apartment, $42,000
- Home health aide $57,000
- Homemaker aide $48,000
- Adult day care community center $17,000

A fully loaded policy, paying $200 per day for a stay of up to five years at a skilled nursing facility, costs around $7000 per year for a healthy 55-year-old man. The payout increases by only 5% compounded each year. A single woman of the same age will pay around $10,500 per year for the same coverage (women generally live longer than men, but that means they may need skilled nursing for longer). These already costly premiums will spike higher each and every year on the "birthday" of the policy. Most people are at first shocked by LTC insurance pricing. But with no long-term-care insurance at all, a catastrophic illness could wipe out your savings.

Most long-term care insurance policies cover a wide range of services offered at home or in a skilled nursing facility, but there are caveats:

1. The policy will require the insured need assistance with dressing and bathing, at a minimum, and/or have diagnosed severe cognitive impairment.
2. Expenses are reimbursed up to a predetermined amount. After that you are on your own.

Most seniors are put off by the high cost of long-term care insurance, and they are especially wary of the volatility of premium payment that always increases well above the inflation rate year-to-year, regardless of the senior's health history and current status. Other seniors may shun long-term care insurance because they feel that, if they do not end up ever using it, they have wasted a lot of money. In the end, most seniors tend to think of long-term care insurance as something only for the wealthy. What should you do if you are not wealthy? The long-term care insurance industry has worked to come up with plans that are more attractive to seniors of ordinary means. Let's take a closer look.

You may be able to pay LTC premiums with a tax-free transfer designated as a "1035 exchange" from the cash value of a life insurance policy or annuity. Other than a 1035 exchange, the only way to reduce LTC insurance premiums is by making tradeoffs. Keep in mind that most long-term care insurance claims begin and end with in-home caregiving and that most long-term care insurance claims end within one year. So, coverage that only pays a maximum of $165,000 per year, with a maximum of 3-years of coverage, may be good enough for most scenarios. Considering the average stay in SNF's is 2-1/2 to 3 years.

It really is best for the average middle class person to view LTC insurance as catastrophic insurance with limited benefits and with a big yearly increase in premiums. People of average means should not view LTC insurance as a way to pay for all of their long-term care.

Try to strike a balance between your need to avoid catastrophe and your budget. Research LTC insurance pricing in your local area, or, if moving to be close to your adult children in the event of the need for residential skilled nursing, ask your adult children to research their local market for pricing. If you would be in a market for insurance with relatively lower LTC costs, (the average cost of a home health aide is $110 per day in your area and a private room in a skilled nursing facility home is $190 a day), consider a LTC insurance policy that pays out a maximum of $140 per day. In the above example, the same 55 year old man will pay around $2000 for $140 a day for coverage, trading off a maximum of five years for a maximum of only three years, and trading off a 5% compound inflation adjustment for a 3% compound inflation adjustment. That less expensive policy would provide up to $153,300 in coverage in today's dollars.

Lessening the inflation adjustment results in the biggest savings. Insurers have drastically raised premiums for 5% inflation protection because their own investments are currently earning low interest rates. In the last five years, assisted living and home care costs have risen 2% a year and residential skilled nursing rates have increased by 4% a year. So you need some inflation protection if you buy coverage in your fifties or sixties and may not need care for 20 years or so, and going from 5% to 3% is a good trade off.

Shortening the benefit period saves money, but this trade-off means that you would not have enough coverage for a degenerative dementia condition.

Couples can buy a shared-benefit policy where instead of a three-year benefit period each, they'd have a pool of six years to use between them. Adding this benefit costs an additional 15% to 22%.

Extending the waiting period can also lower the premium, although you'll have to pay the full cost of care before your insurance covers anything. Policies with a 90-day waiting period tend to offer a good balance, but look for a "calendar day" waiting period. That starts the clock ticking as soon as you qualify for care, either because you need help with two activities of daily living or have cognitive impairment.

A "service day" waiting period has the same benefit trigger but counts only the days you receive care. The average person receives home care 3.5 days per week, according to the American Association for Long-Term Care Insurance (AALTCI). Some insurers charge about 15% extra for a policy with no waiting period for home care.

Annual premiums are lower when you are younger, although you'll pay them longer. The sweet spot, from a risk analysis viewpoint, is for healthy people getting long-term-care insurance is in late 50's to early 60's. It is difficult to qualify for coverage as you near 70 years old. Approximately 20% of people in their 50's who apply for coverage are denied; 30% of those in their sixties and 45% in their seventies were turned down, says the AALTCI.

Most insurers now perform medical exams, which may include cognitive assessments for applicants who are older than 60. Some companies may charge more if you have a family history of early-onset Alzheimer's or heart issues.

It helps to work with an agent who deals with several insurers and knows which ones have the best rates. Some of the best LTC insurance companies:

- American General Life (AIG)
- Bankers Life and Casualty
- Berkshire Life
- Genworth
- John Hancock
- Lincoln Financial Group
- MassMutual
- Mutual of Omaha
- New York Life Insurance Company
- Northwestern Mutual Life Insurance Company
- Prudential Insurance
- State Farm Insurance
- Thrivent For Lutherans
- Transamerica
- Unum US

AARP Long Term Care is not an insurance company and has ceased offering LTC insurance effective June 2013.

Below are The American Association of Long-Term Care Insurance most recent "application declined" data out of a random sampling of around 100,000 applicants...

Percentage of applicants declined for LTC Insurance coverage:

- Below age 50: 14%
- Ages 50-to-59: 21%
- ˙ Ages 60-to-69: 27%
- Ages 70-to-79: 45%

Keep in mind that only the wealthy can afford to start LTC coverage in their mid-60's and beyond. Also, all of the applicants are people who the insurance agent felt had a high chance of qualifying. The agent does not want to waste his or your time. These lower or middle income applicants were rejected after an arduous application process. Some of these lost efforts could be prevented by consulting a care manager with experience doing these kinds of applications.

Using Life Insurance to Fund a Liquidity Crisis or Long-Term Care

Taking cash out of a life insurance policy is typically considered when:

- The policy holder is unable to pay the premiums and is in danger of having their policy lapse
- The policy holder has outlived his or her beneficiaries
- In the event of a severe liquidity crisis

There are several ways to use life insurance as a source of funds to pay for unexpected senior care expenses. Careful analysis, perhaps with an outside professional consultant, of tax consequences and the senior's life circumstances, such as estimated life expectancy, is necessary to correctly choose the optimal method for using life insurance to fund long-term care.

Beside a cash benefit going to survivors of a deceased husband, wife, and/or children, whole life insurance yields, over time, a cash value or accumulation value of interest-earning inflated premiums. This is termed "life insurance cash value."

Death benefit loans come in a lump sum, borrowed from the policy's cash value, and can be used for any purpose. These types of loans will have a low interest rate and no repayment schedule. If not repaid with accrued interest upon the policy-holder's death, the death benefit will be reduced by the amount of the principal on the loan.

A policy holder can take loans withdrawn from the cash reserve, or get the full amount of the reserve through cash surrender of the policy, minus surrender fees and taxes upon cash out. A cash payout and surrender is best for policies with a substantial cash value. Cash surrender should be employed only after careful consideration because it gives up the policy's death benefit, and, depending on the policy-holder's disease history and current health, it may be very expensive to replace this coverage if at all.

Implications to be carefully considered before the decision to sell a life insurance policy include:

- The usually large transaction fees
- Capital gains tax
- If the policy holder dies sooner than anticipated, the loss of tax-free death benefits may negate the value of the cash payout
- If the policyholder dies much later than had been expected they lose their insurance and are probably no longer insurable
- Do you have other assets for a Funeral or Burial?

Hybrid Long-Term Care/Life Insurance Policy

"Hybrid" or a "linked" life insurance policies may be the solution to long-term care insurance for many middle class seniors. The policy holder pays either life insurance premiums or a lump sum annuity to guarantee coverage for long-term care. When long-term care is needed, funds paid out of the policy are not taxed. If the senior dies without ever getting so ill as to require long-term care, death benefits accrue for the policy's beneficiaries.

But hybrid plans do not offer as much coverage as a stand-alone plan, may have higher deductibles, may overlap with Medicare and private insurance, may not cover in-home care, and are often more expensive than a stand-alone long-term care insurance policy.

Deciding whether or not to buy hybrid life insurance is a difficult decision best done with the help of a professional senior care planning consultant. A professional can work with you and your family and friends to write up a custom long-term senior care plan that may or may not include the purchase of hybrid insurance.

Life or Viatical Settlement

Life and viatical settlements are funds provided by third party companies or investors. A long-term life insurance policyholder sells the life insurance to the third party for a lump sum. Life and viatical settlements are nearly the same, except that a viatical settlement is typically used for those with a life expectancy of five years or less. Life settlements make most sense for policies with little or no cash value. These settlements are investments, so they may be bought and sold, though that has no effect on the contract.

These methods yield more cash than the policy's cash surrender value but less than its face value. The third party, known as a "life settlement company," then pays the policy premium until the policyholder's death, upon which they collect the death benefit. Money coming from this "life settlement" can be used for any purpose. It is typically used to remodel the senior's existing a home to make it fall-safe and mobility-friendly, to pay for residency at an assisted living community, or to pay large healthcare bills.

Though opting to get a life or viatical settlement may seem like a fairly simple option to consider, it is not. Capital gains tax must be paid on the difference between the premiums paid and the cash settlement, with a deduction available in many cases if the cash is used to pay-for-long-term care. A consultation and analysis by a tax professional is necessary prior to the decision to take a life or viatical settlement. Also, cash gained from a life settlement or accelerated death benefit may interrupt the recipient's Supplemental Social Security or Medicaid eligibility.

Death benefit loans and accelerated death benefits are for those who wish to preserve benefits for their survivors and who are financially able to continue paying premiums. If you do decide to go for a life settlement, it's well worth your while to pay for the services of a reputable licensed broker who can help make sure you get a fair price for your policy.

Accelerated Death Benefits

An accelerated death benefit (ADB) is for the terminally ill. A policy holder invokes an ADB to receive a portion of the policy's death benefit before their death. Upon the policy holder's death, beneficiaries receive the death benefit minus the amount of the ADB. Prior to death, premiums must still be paid. Accelerated death benefits are not repaid.

Loans

Unsecured Lines of Credit

A checking and debit card bank account often has a line of credit in the form of overdraft protection. Other types of lines of credit are a revolving credit card, personal line of credit, and demand loans. Here we will discuss a special type of credit line intended for people age 62 and over. Typically a line of credit made available for senior care needs is unsecured. This line of credit often requires an adult child or adult children as cosigners.

This type of credit line is termed a **HELOC or** "home equity line of credit". A HELOC is a loan is akin to using a credit card with a very low interest rate. It allows borrowers to pay for care on an as-needed basis. The bank approves a homeowner(s) for a set amount of money with a defined end date. The homeowner can borrow as much as needed whenever needed, up to the preset maximum dollar amount. Monthly payments will go up depending on the amount borrowed and how much borrowed money has already been repaid.

A HELOC is intended to be a short-term solution, filling the gap until other funds are available. Your line of credit can be used to cover the monthly cost of senior living, expenses while you wait to sell your home or apply for a VA benefit.

Securing a HELOC from a bank without putting up any collateral is commonly used for a short-term liquidity crisis brought on by the need for a temporary stay in an assisted living community or skilled nursing facility for defined or closely estimated time period, or to pay off large medical bills. A line of credit has a higher interest rate compared to a home equity loan because it's unsecured. But interest rate is much lower than a credit card. There is usually a one-time origination and support fee added to the principal.

At the end of the loan period, the borrower(s) pays back the loan in a lump sum, including interest, typically by selling the house. However, interest is only paid on the amount that was actually borrowed during the withdrawal period, though there may be a small "unused funds" fee based on the amount that was approved but not used. Turnaround time required to get a line of credit is short, perhaps only a couple days. A HELOC application form allows multiple applicants, so the loan may still be issued even if the senior-in-need's credit score is too low to get the line of credit on their own.

Some examples of situation for which HELOCs are commonly used:

- To be prepared to cover costs in the case of unforeseen or untimely events.
- The senior is in the process of borrowing on a life insurance policy or liquidating part or their entire private investment portfolio to cover the costs of assisted living or skilled nursing care.
- Veteran benefits are being applied for and are expected to be granted.
- You, your parent, or loved one is waiting for the sale of a home to close.

Home Equity Lines of Credit range from $10,000 to $150,000. HELOCs are accepted by most assisted living communities and skilled nursing facilities across the U.S. Once the HELOC is approved, low interest-only payments are made monthly, with the principal due at loan maturity. Borrowers tap the funds at their discretion. Interest accumulates on money withdrawn. The borrower pays an annualized percentage on the money not withdrawn. This is called an "Unused Line Fee." Funds to cover assisted living expenses are then sent directly to the assisted living community or skilled nursing facility.

Benefits of an "Assisted Living Line of Credit" or other-use HELOC:

- HELOC documents stipulate clearly that this is for mom or dad's medical bills, in-home care, or residential housing.

- Helps community application approval process to go smoothly because the application reviewer knows that funds can be sent directly to the community each month.
  There are smaller monthly payments on funds used while you wait for the house to sell at a higher price.
- Credit Line up to $50,000. Plenty of time to sell the home, with flexible repayment terms over 3 - 5 years.
- Same day decision if application is made early in the day, with fast funding (24 to 48 hours). Use only what you need as you need it.
- Up to six persons on the application, so one sibling doesn't have to carry the burden of risk.

Using Home Equity to Pay for Senior Care

There are three ways to draw money out of your home: rent, sell, and borrow.

See the Comparison Table on the following page:

Options for Using a Home to Pay for Care

Marital Status	Type of Care	Rent Home	Sell Home	Reverse Mortgage	HELOC
Single	Home Care	N/A	N/A	Available	Available
Single	Assisted Living	Available	Available	N/A	Available
Single	Skilled Nursing Facility	Available	Available	N/A	Available
Married	Home Care for 1 Spouse	N/A	N/A	Available	Available
Married	Assisted Living for 1 spouse	N/A	N/A	Available	Available
Married	Skilled Nursing Facility for 1 Spouse	N/A	N/A	Available	Available
Married	Both need In Home Care	N/A	N/A	Available	Available
Married	Both in Assisted Living Community	Available	Available	N/A	Available
Married	Both in Skilled Nursing Facility	Available	Available	N/A	Available

Selling the Home

Money resulting from selling a home can be put in the bank or invested. Often, the amount of money is big enough to be used to pay for assisted living or skilled nursing for several years. But in the most common scenario, where life expectancies are unknown or are not predictable enough, this money may run out. One solution available for people holding $600,000 or more is to purchase a lifetime annuity that guarantees a monthly income for one or both spouses for the remainder of their lives, regardless of how long they live.

Medicaid eligibility may be lost upon the sale of the home. Medicaid can often be used to pay for a portion of skill nursing costs. Before a home is sold and when occupied by the homeowner(s), it is not an asset counted when determining Medicaid eligibility. As soon as the home is sold, the remaining money after paying broker fees etc. is now counted by Medicaid as an asset. Now all of that money must be spent down on care costs before eligibility for Medicaid is possible again. If in any doubt, you should consult with a long-term health care planning professional before any decision is made.

Renting the Home

Renting a home can be a good option for paying for assisted living or a skilled nursing facility. Some important considerations:

1. Don't rent your home if you plan to use Medicaid to pay long-term expense. Once you leave the home, it is considered an asset and will likely preclude Medicaid

eligibility, unless you see a financial planner who can set up asset protection for you first.

2. The landlord can be either home owner, though, in the case of skilled nursing, preferably a friend, family member, or a professional property management company hired and monitored by a family member or friend.

3. The house must be in good condition, free of defects that may incur high repair costs.

4. The house must have a low maintenance exterior in good repair, and preferably, low maintenance landscaping and other surroundings

5. The owner must possess clear title or have very low mortgage payments.

6. There must be a ready reserve of cash to handle any period of vacancy.

Assuming a good tenant is paying rent on time and is expected to stay a long time, cash to pay for senior care will then be continuously available. Renting, for example, to a family with school age children, with no more children planned, can help significantly reduce the risk of vacancy. Even better is if the family is supported by a trades or factory job, or a white collar job with a small local company or a local public service, not a "move up the corporate ladder and move to a new city for a larger home" larger corporation.

Secured Line of Credit

A conventional line of credit or an "assisted living secured line of credit" allows you to borrow sums that total no more than the credit limit, similar to a credit card. Collateral, usually in the form of home equity, is required for an assisted living secured line of credit set up for payment to be made to the community where the senior is moving. A secured line of credit may not alternately be tied to an assisted living community, but instead, is used for major expenses like medical bills.

The limit on a line of credit is known as the "allowable line." Lenders make secured lines of credit that max at up to 85% of the value of your home, minus the amount owed, if any. Lenders look at your monthly income, monthly debts and bills, credit score and history, just like they did when you first got a mortgage. Below is an example of how a lender calculates the line of credit limit:

The lender allows a maximum credit limit of up to 70% of the home's value and the home appraise for $360,000. You owe $60,000 on the current mortgage, so you qualify for a credit line amount of up to $105,000. ($360,000 x 70% = $255,000, - $60,000 = $192,000).

The draw period is the date range for which you can pay for expenses with the line of credit; anywhere from 1 - 10 or more years, with ten years being the most common. You'll receive a card or checks to pay for expenses. When paying for assisted living or skilled nursing, you'll receive a monthly bill that you pay for with the line of credit.

Tax deductible interest accumulates on the money borrowed against the line of credit, which has variable interest rate, changing month to month. But the monthly payment depends mostly, as you would expect, on how much how much has been borrowed to date.

Traditional Reverse Mortgages

Borrowers can use a reverse mortgage to receive tax-free payments from a financial institution, instead of borrowing a lump-sum of cash and making monthly payments. Reverse mortgages are a quick and easy way to unlock home equity, though all outstanding liens on the home must be paid off by the reverse mortgage before additional funds can be withdrawn. A reverse mortgage is not due payable until the borrower sells the home or dies. The balance of the loaned money comes due at that time. Any remaining equity goes to the owner(s) or their beneficiaries.

The homeowner retains full ownership of their home. The lending institution owns a simple lien on the property. When the loan comes due, homeowners will never owe more than the fair market value of the house. If the equity is smaller than the amount due for repayment, family members do not have to make up the difference. The loss goes to the lender.

Reverse mortgages are easy to get, requiring only that the applicant(s) must be at least 62 years old, must own clear title or nearly clear title, live in the home as their primary residence, and the home must be a house, condominium, or a permanently fixed mobile or manufactured home on concrete padding. The amount of equity that can be withdrawn from the borrower's home is always something less than the home's full fair market value.

HELOC vs Reverse Mortgage

HELOCs are often considered as an alternative to reverse mortgages to pay for care. Reverse mortgages are loans for seniors over 62 years of age that allow eligible applicants to receive cash using equity they have in their homes. This type of loan has considerable consumer protections built in for the elderly, but there are situations where a HELOC is the better option.

Home Equity Conversion Mortgage (HECM) Loans

Just like a privately funded reverse mortgage, The Federal Housing Administration's Home Equity Conversion Mortgage (HECM) reverse mortgage loan program is available to people age 62 and over who maintain the home as their primary residence, and own clear or nearly clear title to the home. Also, there is a mandatory meeting with a HECM counselor to discuss eligibility requirements and provisions for loan repayment, financial effects of a HECM loan, and an alternative will be suggested by the counselor when the senior would be better served by other means of funding.

The amount of HECM loans is determined by calculating the amount remaining after initial and annual mortgage insurance premiums, an origination fee, various service fees, third-party charges and interest on the loan itself. But these are not out-of-pocket because they can usually be paid with the proceeds of the loan itself. Lenders charge an origination fee as compensation for processing the HECM loan. The fee will range from around $2,000 for homes valued at less than $125,000, up to $4000 on the first $200,000 of a home's value, plus 1% of any amount of home value over $200,000. Origination fees are capped at $6,000. The fees are added to the line of credit, to be paid when the loan is retired.

There are five types of HECM Loans:

1. Tenure - Equal monthly payments for as long as the borrower remains alive and maintains the property as a principal residence.
2. Term - Equal monthly payments made for a fixed period of months selected by the borrower.
3. Line of Credit - Unscheduled payments at a time of the borrower's choosing and in amounts the borrower requests until the line of credit is exhausted.
4. Modified Tenure - Scheduled monthly payments and optional unscheduled payments on demand.
5. Modified Term - Scheduled monthly payments and optional unscheduled payments on demand for a fixed number of months as determined by the borrower.

Funds are transferred electronically to the community at your request each month. A monthly phone call to the designated "family leader" may be required prior to disbursement. The amount you use each month is entirely up to the senior and the family. It does not have to be the same amount each month.

The senior and family must consider the advantages and disadvantages to their specific situation to determine if a home equity line of credit is the preferred source of funding to pay for senior care need.

Pros when choosing a HECM over a traditional reverse mortgage:

- Provides funding for care while determining if the home should be sold.
- No requirement that the homeowner remain living in their home.
- Lower fees compared with a traditional reverse mortgage.
- Flexibility to accommodate sudden increases in their monthly expenses due to the added cost of residential care.
- Flexibility to return to living at home should overall health improve so much as to allow it.

Seniors with immediate care needs often choose to use a HELOC because there is no requirement that they remain living at home. Should circumstances make it necessary for them to move into residential care, their reverse mortgage will not suddenly become due.

Cons when choosing a HECM over a traditional reverse mortgage:

- The borrower's credit score plays an important part in the approval process because monthly payments are expected, whereas with a traditional reverse mortgage the focus is squarely on the fair market value of the home and how much of that value the applicant holds as equity.
- HELOCs are not as tightly regulated as reverse mortgages, so some consumer protection will not apply.
- Unlike a traditional reverse mortgage, a HELOC requires that the homeowner continue to make monthly payments.
- If several payments are missed in a row, the home can be foreclosed.

Conceding the cons, married couples and singles in good health often do not choose to use a HELOC as a means of paying for care because the degree of need for care is largely undetermined at present.

When only one spouse requires residential care, and both spouses are 62 or older, both traditional reverse mortgages and HELOCs can be good options, with expected extent and duration of the care required being the deciding factor when choosing one over the other. A professional long-term care planner should be consulted prior to making a final decision.

Bridge Loans

During times or in places where the home real estate market is "slow," selling a house at a fair price may require having it on the market for a year or more. Bridge loans are used to "bridge the gap" in financing that occurs between the point in time that a move to an assisted living community or skilled nursing facility is made and the house sells. The locked capital can be made liquid with a bridge loan, freeing home equity so that it can be used to pay for, perhaps unanticipated emergencies that require an ill or disabled senior's permanent move into an assisted living community or skilled nursing facility.

Bridge loans are generally designed to be taken out by entire families, even though it is an unsecured loan, a strong credit score may not be required from the senior.

Two examples follow of when a home equity bridge loan is a good solution:

1. An aging couple that are still fit and active in retirement, but are ready to downsize, and, perhaps because of a family history of heart disease, cancer, and/or dementia, want a move to a Continuing Care Retirement Community. This is a combination of independent living, assisted living, and skilled nursing, offering high risk couples the ability to "age in place" together, or at least in relatively close proximity, without worry of becoming a burden on family members. But the couple is shocked to learn about the degree to which Continuing Care Retirement Communities are expensive, requiring upfront

payment from $50,000 to $1 million. Other financial realities become clear, such as the fact that Medicare will cover only a relatively tiny portion of the expenses. They may each hold a long-term care insurance policy, but at present, neither meets the need qualification for placement to draw funds on the policy. So the couple needs a way to fund the move while the house is not selling. The residential real estate market is slow. And, on top of all that, the couple may be patiently waiting for Veteran's Administration benefits to take effect (up to a year or more). A bridge loan would fund the move.

2. A daughter notices that dad is suddenly having much more trouble getting up and down the stairs, or perhaps there has already been an injurious fall, and he needs to move to a skilled nursing facility as soon as possible. The real estate agent informs the family that the home will probably not sell anytime soon, the market is slow, but the senior needs to pay assisted living move-in costs right away. There is a Veteran Aid and Attendance benefit application in process for dad, but the family is unsure of when those funds will become available. A bridge loan would fund the move while the house is still on the market.

A bridge loan application is usually approved or rejected in a week or less. Multiple applicants also make this loan easier to secure by sharing the financial risk, reducing or eliminating the danger that an individual applicant's credit score won't be high enough for this unsecured loan. Typically, up to six family members can share the risk of the loan, especially when one person may not have adequate individual credit. The more co-borrowers that are listed on the loan, the more likely it will be approved.

The health and age of the individual in need of care is not a factor in eligibility, though lenders want to know about any source of income that will become available within a few months or a year, such as the sale of a home or retroactive veterans benefits.

We understand the demands of caring for your loved ones and we can help. We can offer some peace of mind as we go the extra mile. We will support you through the process! We can help you stay fit and financially healthy, and have a better quality of life with the best caregiving options available to you or your loved ones.

Let us get you the help you need so you can stay healthy and happy!

Conclusion

As you see, there is a lot of information to be navigated as one prepares for aging care. I hope this book will be useful to seniors, family members or caregivers facing decisions for care and placement. It is essential to have a care manager involved to provide assistance with resources, applications and the endless communication involved with caring for an aging loved one. **Senior Care of Sacramento** can answer all of your questions or find the resources who can answer them. This book is meant to reduce the confusion around these difficult decisions, by informing seniors and their families about what might be involved with caring for an aging or medically compromised senior, with increasing levels of care needs. This is also meant to encourage caregivers and families that there are resources and financial support available. We need to work together to find the best financial, psychological/emotional and caregiving resources for an aging parent.

Don't hesitate, call us Senior Care of Sacramento at

(916) 877-6904 or visit our website at:
http://seniorcareofsacramento.com.

Appendices

Many of the forms in the Appendices can be downloaded from our website at http://seniorcareofsacramento.com/book.

The password is scosacramento.

Appendix A: Three Page Assessment Form

The 3-page Assessment form can be downloaded from our website here:

http://seniorcareofsacramento.com/client-assessment-form

Therese Johnson/ Gerontologist

Consultant:_____ Eval. Date_____

Client Assessment Form "Top Page"

Client

Name:_____ Age:_____ Date:_____

Address:_____ State:_____ Zip:_____

Cell #:_____ Hm. #:_____ Other #:_____

Responsible Party

Name:_____ Relationship:_____

Address:_____ State:_____ Zip:_____

Cell #:_____ Hm.#:_____ Work #:_____

Fax #:_____ Email: _____

Responsible Party #2:_____

DC Planner:_____ Phone #:_____

Using Other Referral Services:_____ Area Desired:_____

Leaving: ☐Hospital ☐SNF ☐Senior Residence ☐Own Home ☐Relatives home

Est. Start Date:_____ Est. Move-in date:_____

Type of Home: ☐Assisted Living ☐Board & Care ☐Not Sure

Type of Room: ☐Private ☐Shared ☐Studio ☐1 Bedroom ☐2 Bedroom

Financial:

Monthly Income: $_____ Savings: $_____ Budget: $_____/mo

Housing: ☐Own Home ☐Must Sell ☐LTC Ins. Estimated Proceeds: $_____

Government Programs: ☐SSI ☐Medicare Part B ☐Medi-Cal ☐Other:_____

Primary Diagnosis: _____

Comments: _____

_____

_____

_____

_____

_____

_____

101

Senior Care of Sacramento

Client Assessment form

Client Name:_____ Age:_____ Height:_____ Weight:_____ D.O.B: _____

Primary Diagnosis:_____

Cognitive/Behavior	Memory	Mobility/Transfer	Neurological
☐ Alert	☐ Oriented to Name	☐ Independent	☐ No problems Noted
☐ Periods of Agitation	☐ Oriented to Place	☐ Cane	☐ Parkinson's
☐ Periods of Confusion	☐ Month/Year	☐ Walker	☐ Multiple Sclerosis
☐ Anxiety		☐ Wheelchair	☐ RS Weakness
☐ Combative	**Short Term**	☐ -Self Propels	☐ LS Weakness
☐ Sundowner's	☐ Appears Okay	☐ Stand by Assist	☐ Paralysis
☐ Verbally Abusive	☐ Mild Loss	☐ 1 Person Assist	☐ Tia's (mini-strokes)
☐ Requires Redirecting	☐ Moderate Loss	☐ 2 Person Assist	☐ Stroke:
☐ Wander Risk	☐ Severe Loss	☐ Fall Risk	☐ Seizure Disorder
☐ Signs of Depression	**Long Term**	☐ Poor Safety Awareness	
☐ Follows Directions	☐ Appears Okay	Notes_____	
☐ Confusion:	☐ Some Problems	_____	
☐ Physician Diagnosis:		_____	
☐ -Alzheimer's		_____	
☐ -Dementia		_____	

Respiratory	Cardiovascular	Toileting	Bedtime/Sleeping	Feeding
☐ No Problems	☐ No Problems	☐ Independent	☐ Usually Sleeps Thru Night	☐ Feeds Self
☐ Shortness of Breath	☐ CHF	☐ Continent	☐ Irregular Habits	☐ Needs Food Cut
☐ Pneumonia	☐ Angina	☐ Periodic Accidents	☐ Insomnia	☐ Soft Food
☐ COPD	☐ Hypertension (HBP)	☐ Briefs-Day	☐ May Wake to use Toilet	☐ Swallowing issues
☐ Inhaler/Nebulizer	☐ Atrial Fibrillation	☐ Briefs-Night	☐ Toilet 2-3 times	☐ Chewing Issues
☐ Bronchitis/Asthma	☐ Edema	☐ Incontinent-Bladder	☐ Needs Assist Toileting	☐ Own Teeth
☐ Oxygen ☐ 24/7 ☐ PRN	☐ Prior Heart Attack	☐ Incontinent-Dribble	☐ Uses Commode at Night	☐ Dentures
☐ Self-Administered	☐ Prior Bypass	☐ Incontinent-bowel		☐ Appetite:
☐ Needs Help	☐ Pacemaker	☐ Wears Pads		☐ Normal Diet
	☐ Coronary Artery Disease	☐ Needs Urinal		☐ Special Diet (notes)
		☐ Needs Assistance Toileting		☐ Food Allergies

Notes_____

Bathing	Groom/Dress	Hearing	Vision	Diabetes
☐ Independent	☐ Independent	☐ Adequate	☐ Adequate	☐ None
☐ Verbal Cueing	☐ Verbal Cueing	☐ Fair	☐ Fair	☐ Controlled by Diet
☐ Stand-by Assist	☐ Stand-by Assist	☐ Poor	☐ Poor	☐ Oral Medication
☐ Hands-on Assist	☐ Hands-on Assist	☐ Wears Aids	☐ Glasses	☐ Self-Managed Insulin
☐ -Light	☐ -Layout Clothes		☐ Glaucoma	☐ Assist w/insulin
☐ -Moderate	☐ -Assist shaving		☐ Cataracts	☐ Self-Monitoring
☐ -Total	☐ Dental assistance		☐ Past Surgery	☐ Assist Monitoring
Notes:_____			☐ Macular Degeneration	
_____			☐ Legally Blind	

Senior Care of Sacramento

Client Assessment form

Client Name:_____

Skin Care	**Other (Medical)**	**Other**	**Urinary/Ostomy**
☐ Routine care	☐ Arthritis	☐ Smoker (no. a day_____)	☐ Self-Manage Foley
☐ Ointment for Skin	☐ Osteoporosis	☐ Alcohol Abuse	☐ Catheter – Temp_____
☐ Bruises	☐ Fractures	☐ History of Drug Abuse	☐ Assist Emptying Bag
☐ Bruises Easily	☐ Medical Procedures Pending		☐ Self-Manage Ostomy
☐ Dermal	☐ On Hospice		☐ Assistance with Ostomy
☐ Stage:_____			☐ Urinary Tract Infection
Notes_____			

_____

Medications: ☐ Separate Page Attached   Drug Allergies: ☐ Yes   ☐ None Known

_____   _____   _____   _____
_____   _____   _____   _____
_____   _____   _____   _____
_____   _____   _____   _____

Dementia/Behavior Medications:_____

Primary Care Physician:_____   Family advised about Physician's report   ☐ Yes ☐ No

Address:_____   Family Advised about TB test: ☐ Yes ☐ No

_____

Financial:

Have durable power of attorney for: ☐ Health Care   ☐ Financial   ☐ Obtaining   ☐ Conservator

Responsible Party #1:   Responsible Party #2

Name:_____   Name:_____

Address:_____   Address:_____

_____   _____

_____   _____

_____

Client's Budget: ☐ SSI   ☐ Adequate   ☐ Other:

$_____/month   _____

Client Miscellaneous:

Marital Status: _____ Date Of Birth: _____ Occupation:_____

Who takes to medical appointments: ☐ Facility   ☐ Family   ☐ Either   ☐ Veteran   ☐ Spouse of Veteran

☐ Applying for aid and attendance benefits

Client social and activity interests:_____

_____

_____

_____ Pg.3of3

Appendix B: Two Articles: Is it Time to Move Into Assisted Living? And Beginning the Search for Residential Care Housing

IS IT TIME TO MOVE INTO ASSISTED LIVING?

Usually, families and seniors begin to consider alternatives when it becomes difficult for the elderly family member to carry on with important activities of daily living without support and assistance from others. There are many variables and each situation is unique.

Here are a few common reasons for which a decision to move into assisted living is made:

• If the senior lives far from family, moving into assisted living may make sense simply to head off potentially dangerous isolation during a worst-case scenario, such as an earthquake, flood, or power outage of several days due to a weather event.

• A physician prescribes a move into assisted living upon determining that the senior cannot be left unattended due to a health condition requiring frequent or constant monitoring.

• Poor balance, dizziness, bad joints, and weak bones are putting the senior at high risk a fall injury. An environment constructed to minimize risk of falls and help with walking may become essential to prevent injury.

• An increase in certain "special care needs" such as wandering, incontinence, sleeplessness, tube feeding, combative and other difficult dementia behavior, assistance with transferring such as moving from a chair to the bed, or chronic need for skin care treatments.

• Memory loss and forgetfulness, especially when Alzheimer's disease or dementia is diagnosed, becomes dangerous. The senior may forget they have food cooking on the stove, they may forget to eat, or they may forget to take medication or accidentally double doze on medication.

• Loneliness had led to depression resulting loss of motivation for activity and personal care. Living in an assisted living community can alleviate loneliness.

• The senior can no longer attend adult day care, requiring the family to provide care around the clock.

• A medical crisis or hospitalization requires a period of rehabilitation.

• A decline in the physical health of the caregiver spouse or other family member.

Some red flags that indicate that it may be time for a move to assisted living:

• Unpaid bills lying around, possibly due to any of a number of reasons, including cognitive impairment, fatigue, or depression.

It is especially important to be sure the senior is paying insurance bills.

Watch for thank-you messages from charities, especially ones asking for more money. Scam charities, and even some otherwise reputable charities, prey on older adults who have lost some cognitive function that used to enable them to be fiscally prudent. They may even forget how many times they have donated to a particular charity, donating repeatedly over a relatively short period of time.

• Accumulation of unread magazines indicating fatigue or a loss of cognitive function.

• Spoiled food in the refrigerator.

• Unexplained weight loss, perhaps due to inability to prepare meals or do grocery shopping.

• Unexplained weight gain, possibly due to an injury slowing the person down, general frailty, diabetes, or dementia where the senior doesn't remember eating and indulges in meals and snacks, or perhaps even money troubles that limit food choices to bread and pasta.

• You discover that your parent is covering up a bruise from a fall that he or she doesn't want you to see or know about.

• Disheveled appearance that may include unbrushed teeth, unwashed hair, misapplied makeup, wearing the same clothes all the time, leaving button holes left unbuttoned, and uncharacteristic facial hair or forgetting to shave.

• Vision has deteriorated to the point where ability to navigate within the household is impaired or there is a dangerous likelihood of errors in taking medications.

• Dirty kitchen with stale, expired, or spoiled food. Also, multiples of the same item like cereal or ketchup my reveal that the senior, while grocery shopping, is forgetting what they have in stock at home.

• Smell of smoke, a discarded pot or pan, or other sign of a cooking accident or kitchen fire.

• Dirty bathroom.

• Household clutter and unlaundered clothes.

• Untended lawn and plants.

• Unexplained dent or damaged bumper on the car.

• Entrance door left unlocked or open.

• Frequent complaints of loneliness or depression. Be mindful that when a friend has stopped visiting due to health problems or death, the senior may not only become lonely or depressed, but they also become more vulnerable to many other problems that otherwise would have been noticed and corrected.

• Chronic sleep loss.

• Uncharacteristic mood swings, or combative and other difficult dementia behavior.

• Medical scares happening with increasing frequency and/or slow recovery from medical problems.

• Missed appointments, dropping out of a club, missing social events, no longer taking an evening walk, not visiting the library anymore, etc.

Source: http://seniorcareofsacramento.com/beginning-the-search-for-residential-care-housing

BEGINNING THE SEARCH FOR RESIDENTIAL CARE HOUSING

The goal when searching for and choosing residential care housing is to get it right the first time, without becoming trapped in "analysis paralysis" and postponing a decision for too long out of fear of making the wrong choice. You must balance optimism with the realism, knowing that you or your loved one's current care needs may not match anticipated needs as aging progresses. Strive to choose a community that is equipped to provide care now and in the future.

The size of a residential care housing establishment can range in size from a small "board and care home" tucked into a residential neighborhood (also termed a "Residential Care Facility for the Elderly" or "RCFE"), caring for five or six residents, up to a large self-contained Assisted Living Community of 60 residents or more. A larger facility will often offer a greater variety of care levels and options, so an Assisted Living Community may be the best choice for a spousal couple who want to stay together over time, even as each spouse's health and other care needs may change dramatically over time.

Other than the size of the community, the determining factors in selecting residential care housing for yourself or a loved one should be:

1. Care needs at the time of the move.
2. Care needs anticipated over time after the move, preferably informed with a medical doctor's prognosis.
3. Budget.
4. Location.

Carefully consideration must be given to health issues that you, your spouse, or your parent has now, as well as health issues that may likely develop or get worse over time. A "health care needs prognosis" or "best guess" that the senior's physician and medical specialists have outlined regarding what support may be needed in the future is very helpful. This should include a plan for an increasing need for memory care if there is already some cognitive impairment or diagnosed dementia. It is much better for everyone involved to choose a community that can handle future needs rather than having to move to another community, starting the whole process over again.

When the time comes that the need for a move to residential care housing is obvious, have the senior's physician complete a "physician's report for community care facilities" form.

Find your local Long-term Care Ombudsman at www.eldercare.gov. They will tell you about any local senior housing communities that have a history of violations or substandard care.

Then enlist the help of a 'senior advocate,' a knowledgeable senior living placement and referral professional who establishes a long-term care plan and shows you the residential care facilities in the area. Many senior care placement agencies are managed by a geriatric care planning expert who can provide an assessment as well as assistance with managing the situation, including crisis management, interviewing in-home help, as well as placement when the time comes. A professional local placement expert can evaluate the senior's care needs, help define budget, and provide tours of licensed RCFEs and Assisted Living Communities that fit the senior's situation. These professional services are free as long as the agency is able to make a placement within a certain time frame, usually 90 days.

Distant family members may want the senior to move close by so that they can better coordinate care and visit often. Planning early, well before a move is necessitated, and especially if the senior will be making a long-distance move to be close to family, will lessen stress and help the process go much more smoothly.

A trial run respite stay at a care facility may lessen the senior's fear when the time comes for a permanent move. A respite stay is a good way to get a feel for a community before making a big commitment. A short stay gives the senior a chance to get comfortable with a choice that with which they were initially not comfortable.

Higher priced residential care housing provides apartment-style living with a scaled-down kitchen. Mid-priced board & care homes provide private rooms in a house in a residential neighborhood, while lower priced board & care homes require each senior in the house to share a room with another senior. All residential care housing has a group dining area and a common area for social and recreational activities. Pricing for residential care housing for seniors with dementia is much higher.

Don't hesitate to ask questions and record observations during senior housing tours. Ask each RCFE owner or Assisted Living Community administrator for a brochure, sample menu, activity/social calendar, admission agreement, and housing rules list. Discuss your impressions with the placement agency and with the senior being placed, family members, and other interested parties. Ask the facility everyone favors for placement to evaluate the senior for their assessment of placement suitability. Get a notebook and make notes as you tour each facility and also in the parking lot after you leave the building.

Do not judge residential care facilities by their outside facades and interior luxury. Polished ambience is nice but not necessary. Clean and tidy is enough. A beautiful luxury building may be given daily care to keep new patients coming in, but caregivers in that building may not be focused on the most important aspect of choosing residential care housing: caregiver experience and empathy. Look for housing staffed by enthusiastic and experienced caregivers, and populated by residents who are smiling and happy. Ask for references and check them. Speak to the residents. Note their appearance and how the staff interacts with them. Speak privately with staff about their level of satisfaction.

Ask both residents and staff about the bulletin board listing daily activities. A vibrant activity program can slow an aging senior's deterioration. Are the activities always actually done? If not, how often are activities cancelled or delayed? The meals might seem "gourmet" in the brochure, but actually are high calorie, low fiber, and low protein. Ask residents about this. If you see family visiting, stop and talk to them. If the community claims to have a nurse on staff, talk to that nurse to be sure they are always on-call and available.

Location is important but not a deal breaker. The intention of visiting a parent every day does not often result in consistent daily visits. Life gets in the way. When a better housing option is a couple miles further, go with the best fit.

Check the housing and care contract for additional fees and price increases. Some communities charge one fee for room and board, and a separate fee for care. Other communities charge individually for each service or they may determine the level of care that a resident needs and charge accordingly. Some communities provide all-inclusive pricing.

Loss of independence can be depressing for the senior having to move to residential care housing. When considering a move away from a senior's home and into a residential care facility, it is important for the senior and their family to keep in mind that this event, though often sad and stressful, may actually reduce loneliness as it will likely lead to new experiences, new friendships, and finding new interests never considered before. Be mindful that care received in the Residential Care Facility for the Elderly board and care home or an Assisted Living Community may actually prolong the senior's ability to maintain at least some of their overall feelings of independence and well-being that in actuality would have been lost staying at home alone. Moving to residential care housing may negate the need for nursing home care later on.

This article can also be found on our website at: http://seniorcareofsacramento.com/beginning-the-search-for-residential-care-housing

Appendix C: The Companion Worksheet

The Comparison Worksheet
This worksheet can be found on our website at:
http://seniorcareofsacramento.com/comparison-worksheet-
for-assisted-living-board-and-care

COMPARISON WORKSHEET

Compare the cost of living in your home with living at an Assisted Living or Board & Care. When you add it up, you may be surprised to find that living in a care home is less costly. Additional charges for a second person living in the same care home will apply.

AVERAGE MONTHLY EXPENSE	YOUR HOME	ASSISTED LIVING or BOARD & CARE
Basic Cable	$_____	INCLUDED
Food	$_____	INCLUDED
Home Maintenance	$_____	INCLUDED
Housekeeping/Linen Service	$_____	INCLUDED
Internet	$_____	INCLUDED
Mortgage/Rent	$_____	$_____
Property Taxes/Insurance	$_____	N/A
Utilities (gas, electric, water, garbage)	$_____	INCLUDED
Security and 24-hour staff	$_____	INCLUDED
Storage	$_____	$_____
Transportation	$_____	INCLUDED
Yard Maintenance	$_____	INCLUDED
Wellness Program	$_____	INCLUDED
Other	$_____	$_____
MONTHLY COST	$_____	$_____
Subtract Home Equity Earnings (@ 5% interest)	$_____	N/A
TOTAL MONTHLY COST	$_____	$_____

Therese Johnson
(530) 305 8872

Appendix D: The Mini Mental Test

The Mini Mental Tests can be downloaded from our website at:

http://seniorcareofsacramento.com/mini-mental-test-page-1

http://seniorcareofsacramento.com/mini-mental-test-page-2

Mental Status Questionnaire

Senior Care OF SACRAMENTO

This questionnaire is used to assess residents who have been diagnosed with any form of Dementia. While no specific score would exclude a resident, the resident's mental ability is a factor to be considered in combination with their physical and emotional needs.

Max. Score   Resident's Score

5 _____

4 _____

ORIENTATION

What is the (year)(season)(date)(day)(month)?

Where are we (state)(country)(city)(facility)?

REGISTRATION

3 _____

Name 3 common objects ("apple" "table" "penny"). Take 1 second to say each. Then ask the resident to repeat all three. Give 1 second to say each, 1 point for each correct answer. If they don't get all 3, repeat them again.

ATTENTION AND CALCULATION

5 _____

Spell the word "WORLD" backwards. OR, Serial 7's

backwards. Stop after 5 answers.

(D)___(L)___(R)___(O)___(W)___

RECALL

5 _____

Ask for the three common objects named during

Registration above. Give 1 point for each correct answer.

LANGUAGE

2 _____

Show and have the resident name a "pencil" & "watch".

1 _____

Repeat the following sentence "No if, ands, or buts".

3 _____

Follow a 3-stage command: "Take a paper in your right

hand, fold it in half, and put it on the floor."

1 _____

Write a sentence:

1 _____   **Fill in the Clock. Then show 3:00**

Max score possible: 29   Resident's score_____

29-21: Intact to mild Intellectual impairment
20-10: Moderate Intellectual impairment
Less than 9: Severe intellectual impairment

Resident's Name _____   Date _____

Appendix E: Two E-Books: 10 Things You Absolutely Need to Know to Find the Best Care For Your Aging Parents and 10 Frequently Asked Questions for Caregivers

10 Things you absolutely need to know to find the best care for your aging parents.

#1 What is Assisted Living? Assisted Living is a service that provides seniors assistance with their care needs that are related to daily activities of living, such as bathing, dressing, grooming, ambulation, transportation, meals, medication management and housekeeping. This is provided in addition to their housing and utilities.

#2 What's the difference between Board and Care, Assisted Living, and Residential Care?

These three terms are used to describe care assisted living. All three can provide the same level of care. They are interchangeable terms used for describing assisted-living.

In this industry, the term *"Board and Care"* is usually used to differentiate a small, up to 6 bed care home from the larger facilities that may call themselves:

- Residential care communities

- Residential care facilities
- Senior care living
- Assisted living facilities
- Assisted living communities

The larger places (50 to 100 beds) usually consist of more apartment-style living. Some give you options for sharing an apartment/room or a private small studio apartment.

The smaller 6 bed care homes are just that, a private single family home in a residential neighborhood. They provide more home-style living with a roommate situation You can have a shared room or private room in a small 6 bed care home.

Whether you choose a large facility or small -6 Bed care home, they all offer the same amenities and the same services as far as assistance with bathing, dressing, grooming, meals, transportation and medication management.

The smaller 6 bed care homes are better for people who cannot ambulate or walk very far without assistance; because of the home style setting the furthest your senior will need to walk is from their bedroom to the dining room.

In a home style setting, most can manage the small area whereas in large facilities there may be long hallways, elevators and double doors to navigate getting to the dining room.

The biggest benefit I see in a smaller setting type of care, is the homey feeling and better attention from caregivers. With a few other roommates, your senior may experience better independence and a homey feeling.

An advantage of a larger facility is in more activity programs for seniors. They tend to have an Activity Director who can fill the week with lots of entertaining activities to create a community among the residents. Socialization, or potential feeling of belonging to a group is a healthy benefit and provides opportunities for bettering communication, having more fun, and working out differences.

When Facing big decisions regarding which home care works best for your aging family member, we can offer a free evaluation and consultation as to which facility fits your budget and the overall goal that you may have. This reduces time having to research which facility are available or have vacancies. Finding the right budget for the long term can also be daunting.

Senior Care of Sacramento can help customize and find the best suited place for your loved one.

#3 Do assisted living communities have to be licensed?

No matter whether a place is called a board and care, assisted living or residential care they are all governed by the Department of Social Services and the same state licensing regulatory provisions under Title 22.

#4 Does Medicare or MediCal / Medicaid pay for Board and Care , Residential Care Facilities for the Elderly (RCFE), Assisted Living Facilities or Communities?

No. Because these are not medical facilities, neither Medicare nor MediCal/Medicaid pays directly for the residential care/assisted living. There is a MediCal Assisted Living Waiver Pilot Project (ALW) for assisting residents with low-incomes, but there is usually a waiting list and currently they only take high-functioning residents. (L.A., Sacramento, San Joaquin counties)

#5 How does an Assisted-living ,RCFE or Board and Care Home differ from a Skilled Nursing home (SNF)?

Skilled nursing facilities require a licensed medical nurse and doctor to care for your senior, and care correlates to the person's diagnosis. To get the best possible care, we can help by determining if your diagnosis prohibits you from choosing assisted living or a skilled nursing home.

If someone is bedridden (meaning they are in bed the majority of their waking day) they are usually required to be in a skilled nursing home, unless they are on Hospice. They may be eligible for an Assisted Living/RCFE that has an opening for a Hospice resident depending on the person's diagnosis. We can determine eligibility after a customized assessment and is determined on an individual basis.

#6 What does an assisted living community typically cost?

The average monthly cost is $3,500 but could be as high as $5,000 to $6,000, depending on accommodations (e.g., private or shared room), geographic area, level of care need, special care services for dementia or Hospice. We are able to include more affordable assisted-living options if someone is higher functioning and only needs assistance with minimal daily activities of living (bathing, dressing, and grooming). Some places have extra fees for administering medication, Pre-admission, and community fees. Some of these other fees are negotiable and we can help with that as well.

#7 Who is best suited for assisted-living community?

Seniors who are looking for activities and companionship in addition to assistance with their care needs of daily living i.e. bathing, dressing, grooming, ambulation may prefer such a facility. Seniors who are outgoing and enjoy socializing with their peers may prefer an assisted living community.

#8 I don't think it is safe for my loved one to drive; what should I do?

Are you concerned about your loved one's capacity to be driving? Are you wondering if she is safe on the road? Is he a danger to himself or others? The best way to handle this is to speak to their doctor who can assist you with testing them to see if they should be driving or not. You can make a request at their doctor's office. The doctor is a mandated reporter and responsible for submitting a notice to DMV if your loved one failed the test. This keeps you from being put in the middle of the issue, takes it out of your hands and can give you peace of mind.

Give us a call and we assess what the best options to choose at 916-877-6904.

#9 What kinds of services do in-home service agencies offer?

There are two types of in-home service agencies. One offers medical care services and the other offers non-medical homecare services. We can help you to determine whether your loved one needs medical or non-medical services.

#10 My loved one has dementia. Can he receive care in an Assisted Living/ RCFE/ Board and Care?

Yes. Some Assisted Living/RCFE & Board and Cares specialize in dementia care. These Assisted Living/ RCFE/ Board and Care Facilities must meet certain requirements, including training for staff and administrators. Ask about their philosophy of dementia care, and the qualifications of staff and their training program. Of course, with our direct contact and close experiences with these types of facilities, we can recommend the best experienced dementia care facilities to you as well. This report was written from my extensive research and experiences with elder care. Feel free to call, and we would love to chat with you to discuss your concerns and level of urgency--916-877-6904. You don't have to tackle this big decision alone, we are friendly and love to help.

Visit us at our website
http://www.Seniorcareofsacramento.com or you can call us
for a FREE Consultation with our senior care specialist;
Therese Johnson 916-877-6904.

10 Frequently Asked Questions for Caregivers

#1 How do I know if it is time to move into assisted living and my family member or loved one can no longer live at home?

Usually, families and seniors begin to consider alternatives when it becomes difficult for the elderly family member to carry on with important activities of daily living without support and assistance from others. There are many variables and each situation is unique.

Here are a few common reasons for which a decision to move into assisted living is made:

• If the senior lives far from family, moving into assisted living may make sense simply to head off potentially dangerous isolation during a worst case scenario, such as an earthquake, flood, or power outage of several days due to a weather event.

• A physician prescribes a move into assisted living upon determining that the senior cannot be left unattended due to a health condition requiring frequent or constant monitoring.

• Poor balance, dizziness, bad joints, and weak bones are putting the senior at high risk a fall injury. An environment constructed to minimize risk of falls and help with walking may become essential to prevent injury.

• An increase in certain "special care needs" such as wandering, incontinence, sleeplessness, tube feeding, combative and other difficult dementia behavior, assistance with transferring such as moving from a chair to the bed, or chronic need for skin care treatments.

• Memory loss and forgetfulness, especially when Alzheimer's disease or dementia is diagnosed, becomes dangerous. The senior may forget they have food cooking on the stove, they may forget to eat, or they may forget to take medication or accidentally double dose on medication.

• Loneliness had led to depression resulting loss of motivation for activity and personal care. Living in an assisted living community can alleviate loneliness.

• The senior can no longer attend adult day care, requiring the family to provide care around the clock.

• A medical crisis or hospitalization requires a period of rehabilitation.

• A decline in the physical health of the caregiver spouse or other family member.

Some red flags that indicate that it may be time for a move to assisted living:

• Unpaid bills lying around, possibly due to any of a number of reasons, including cognitive impairment, fatigue, or depression.

• It is especially important to be sure the senior is paying insurance bills.

• Watch for thank-you messages from charities, especially ones asking for more money. Scam charities, and even some otherwise reputable charities, prey on older adults who have lost some cognitive function that used to enable them to be fiscally prudent. They may even forget how many times they have donated to a particular charity, donating repeatedly over a relatively short period of time.

• Accumulation of unread magazines indicating fatigue or a loss of cognitive function.

• Spoiled food in the refrigerator.

• Unexplained weight loss, perhaps due to inability to prepare meals or do grocery shopping.

• Unexplained weight gain, possibly due to an injury slowing the person down, general frailty, diabetes, or dementia where the senior doesn't remember eating and indulges in meals and snacks, or perhaps even money troubles that limit food choices to bread and pasta.

• You discover that your parent is covering up a bruise from a fall that he or she doesn't want you to see or know about.

• Disheveled appearance that may include unbrushed teeth, unwashed hair, misapplied makeup, wearing the same clothes all the time, leaving button holes left unbuttoned, and uncharacteristic facial hair or forgetting to shave.

• Vision has deteriorated to the point where ability to navigate within the household is impaired or there is a dangerous likelihood of errors in taking medications.

• Dirty kitchen with stale, expired, or spoiled food. Also, multiples of the same item like cereal or ketchup my reveal that the senior, while grocery shopping, is forgetting what they have in stock at home.

• Smell of smoke, a discarded pot or pan, or other sign of a cooking accident or kitchen fire.

• Dirty bathroom.

• Household clutter and unlaundered clothes.

• Untended lawn and plants.

• Unexplained dent or damaged bumper on the car.

• Entrance door left unlocked or open.

• Frequent complaints of loneliness or depression. Be mindful that when a friend has stopped visiting due to health problems or death, the senior may not only become lonely or depressed, but they also become more vulnerable to many other problems that otherwise would have been noticed and corrected.

• Chronic sleep loss.

• Uncharacteristic mood swings, or combative and other difficult dementia behavior.

• Medical scares happening with increasing frequency and/or slow recovery from medical problems.

• Missed appointments, dropping out of a club, missing social events, no longer taking an evening walk, not visiting the library anymore, etc.

Senior Care of Sacramento helps family caregivers put systems into place which help to avoid a crisis. Examples include the hiring of an in-home health aide, Meals on Wheels, adult day services, and a personal emergency response system in order to help keep your loved one safe.

We can also make recommendations for creating a safe environment for your loved one, such as modifying the bathroom with grab bars and removing slip and fall risky throw rugs.

Reassure your loved one that these services will keep him or her at home safely.

If you're loved one is cognitively impaired or has dementia and you worry about his or her safety, please contact us. We can customize a long-term care plan for your loved one so that, in case a crisis does occur, you'll have the information you need about community and other services in order to make good decisions about your loved one's future.

#2 How much does In-Home Care cost?

Many people are under the impression that Medicare and/or Medicaid will pay for care of an aging relative. Medicare has very limited benefits to cover longterm care needs, either in at home or in an assisted living community or nursing home. MediCal, like Medicaid, is a California state-funded program typically for low-income persons, pays for partial costs of in-home and nursing homecare as long as the senior's income is low enough to qualify for benefits.

The majority of costs associated with the chronic illness or disabilities of senior's are assumed by the family and/or the loved one's own private resources, or private insurance if they have long-term care insurance.

Generally the average family caregiver for someone 50 years or older spends well over $5000 per year on out-of-pocket caregiving expenses. This does not include the actual cost of time spent caring for an aging family member.

A large number of seniors depend on help from trained professionals and home health aides to assist with personal care such as bathing, dressing, meal preparation, medication management, transportation, and light housekeeping.

Currently the average cost of a home health aide is $10-$12 an hour and the cost of hiring home health aides through an agency with licensed, bonded screened caregivers will be higher - somewhere in the range of $25 per hour in California.

Care is often needed 24 hours per day, and that can add up.

If you choose to hire a home health aide privately, we recommend you check with your homeowner's insurance agent to ensure there is adequate coverage for an in-home employee and with the IRS about tax implications. We recommend you consider using an In-home Health service that provides thorough background checks so that you avoid issues with the home health aide being untrustworthy or lazy, becoming frequently ill, quitting, or otherwise just doesn't work out.

You can purchase monthly subscriptions from companies that offer medication reminders and a personal emergency response system. These services cost $20-$90 per month or higher, depending on the service plan.

Meals on Wheels are available on a sliding fee scale depending on the senior's income.

Adult day services, which are very limited to a very few areas, cost from $60 per day and higher. Some include transportation.

The average cost of a semi-private room in a nursing home or skilled nursing facility in California is $265.00 a day and up, depending on the area and the senior's care needs.

The average length of stay in a nursing home is two-and-a-half years. After the first 30 to 90 days, the senior pays a share of costs based on their income.

Medicare provides coverage for a short-term rehabilitation stay in a nursing home or to recover from a hospitalization, but for only as long as they are making progress in their rehabilitation.

Room and board in an assisted living facility, residential care facility, or board and care home may cost more than $40,000 annually. In addition to the cost of room and board in nursing homes and assisted living facilities, seniors also assume the cost of medications supplies and personal care items.

We can create a long-term care plan to help you explore ways to finance care and services. We can also help you with executing important documents such as power of attorney forms for healthcare and finances for seniors.

#3 Am I able to be the caregiver for my loved one or am I up for this?

Typically the family caregiver is a daughter or daughter-in-law who, in addition to household chores and managing finances, may work outside the home, with children to raise.

Everyone has his or her limits as a caregiver. It's important to respect yours.

You are responsible for providing a safe and healthy living environment whether that's in your home, their home, or an assisted living or nursing home.

It's important to remember that it's impossible to do it all. That's where Senior Care of Sacramento can help you find support from your family's friend, healthcare professionals, community services, and volunteers to fill the void.

#4 How long can I expect to be caregiving for my senior?

Most family caregivers expect to be caregiving for at least five years, with many anticipating having to do it for 10 or more years.

Carefully consider the senior's financial resources, your emotional resources, and your community's resources. We can help in this long-term commitment by creating a long-term care plan for your senior, and connecting you to services and resources that make long-term caregiving doable.

#5 If I don't like an in-home health aide or volunteer or nurse that an agency sends me, am I stuck with them?

Absolutely not! Call the agency and speak with the supervising social worker, explain your concerns and ask for suggestions. Personality conflicts can happen and the supervisor will work with you to find a caregiver that best meets your and your senior's needs.

#6 I am so depressed. I didn't realize I would feel this way! What can I do?

Caregiving is a depressing experience. You are grieving losses suffered by the senior, the family, and yourself. It is important to find support, unburden your load and to have a day off regularly. Many family caregivers overlook this important part of their experience.

Call us and we will put you in touch with support groups in your area.

#7 What is respite care?

Respite care allows caregivers to have a brief break or vacation from caregiving.

Some assisted-living facilities provide this short-term care anywhere from one week to a month or more.

You can also receive respite care by having a caregiver come into your home to take care of your loved one while you leave on vacation, or just go away for the weekend.

We can help you find the facilities/Care Homes that provide respite care or we can assist you in getting professional caregivers to come in, and is based on the senior's budget and care needs.

#8 What are my obligations?

You're obligated to protect your senior from physical, emotional, and financial abuse, and to generally provide a safe and healthy living environment. A signed durable power of attorney for healthcare allows a responsible party to make financial and healthcare decisions on behalf of a family member or friend, if that family member or friend is no longer able to make such decisions.

If you do not have this document for an aging relative please contact us for a consult as soon as possible. We can provide these documents to you.

#9 How do I take care of myself and provide care for another?

In order to effectively manage this experience you must take time for yourself daily, weekly, monthly and yearly. Astonishingly, 65% of caregivers die before the person they're caring for due to the stress! If you don't take care of yourself who will take care of your loved one?

When you take regular breaks, you can cope with the stresses, myriad decisions and responsibilities. Otherwise the situation can become unbearable for your senior and your family.

Seniors can make you feel guilty when they need more than you can provide, which only makes things worse when you're already carrying around enough guilt.

Does your senior expect you to make him or her happy? That's not your job. Does your partner or spouse complain that you don't have enough time for them because you are caring for your senior?

We can help you plot out a compromise so that you have a workable schedule for your senior, yourself, and your spouse. It's important to ask for and receive help so you can minimize your guilt.

#10 Who can I contact for help?

Senior Care of Sacramento can create a long-term-care plan and help you determine what you want and need each week, then provide you with referrals to vetted services for help.

We can help you save time, energy, and money by directing you to the correct services for customizing the loved one's needs.

Do you have more questions? For example, is your loved one driving and you know it's not safe but you don't know what to do about it? Call us - we can advise you on how to correct this situation.

We will help you to obtain in-home health services in your area. We can help you find the appropriate assisted-living, board and care, or residential community, in the geographical area you prefer, that fits your senior's budget, and that also meets their needs whether they are diabetic, on oxygen, have dementia, or just looking for an Independent Living community that provides transportation, activities and socialization.

We can also assist you in preparing Power of Attorney documents for healthcare, finding veteran benefits and other financial resources, and suggest community services customized to your individual needs and circumstances.

Contact us now - we will lighten your caregiving burden quickly! 916-877-6904.

Appendix F: Forms to Download: Power of Attorney For Finances, Advanced Health Care Directive and Physician's Report Form

These forms can be downloaded from our website as follows:

Power of Attorney For Finances
http://seniorcareofsacramento.com/durable-power-of-attorney

Advanced Health Care Directive
http://seniorcareofsacramento.com/advance-health-care-directive

Physician's Report Form
http://seniorcareofsacramento.com/physicians-report-form

Appendix G: Skilled Care Answers For Californians

This article can also be found on our website at:

http://seniorcareofsacramento.com/skilled-care-answers-for-californians/

The Bad News:

- Watch out -- paying for skilled care will bankrupt you! Skilled care in California is expensive; $9000+ per month. It is the leading cause of bankruptcy in California.
- The state of California will put a lien on your assets and try to take them even if you have a standard living trust. You are not shielded from loss of assets to the state of California! Your house is an exempt asset for entitlement qualification, but the state of California will still record a lien on your house and try to take it unless you protect it by following the complex rules.

The Good News:

- Neither a big income or large net worth will disqualify you from entitlement benefits for skilled care.
- The 3-year look-back period does not automatically disqualify you. There are ways to negate it. Consult with an expert!

Appendix H: Medicaid "Look Back Period" and Why Geriatric Case Management Pays for Itself

MEDICAL EXPENSE DEDUCTIONS FOR ASSISTED LIVING COSTS

Medicaid "Look Back Period"
http://seniorcareofsacramento.com/medicaid-look-back-period

Why Geriatric Case Management Pays for Itself
http://seniorcareofsacramento.com/geriatric-care-management-pays-for-itself/

Resources and Links

To view these websites, articles, radio interviews and resource links go to this website:

http://www.SeniorCareOfSacramento.com/book and enter **password**: scosacramento

Look for the title of the resource below and click on it to view the information or resource.

Articles

A Reiki Hospice Experience:

http://www.seniorcareofsacramento.com/free-downloads/articles/a-reiki-Hospice-experience/

Experiences of a Reiki Therapist

http://www.seniorcareofsacramento.com/free-downloads/articles/experiences-of-a-reiki-therapist/

Reversing and Holding Alzheimer 's Disease in Remission

http://www.seniorcareofsacramento.com/free-downloads/articles/reversing-and-holding-alzheimers-disease-in-remission-articles

Federal Low Income Housing program also known as the Assisted Living Waiver Program or ALW

Assisted Living Waiver:

www.dhcs.cs.gov/services/ltc/pages/AssistedLivingWaiver.aspx

Treating Alzheimer's disease with Reiki:

http://www.seniorcareofsacramento.com/free-downloads/articles/treating-alzheimers-disease-with-reiki/

Radio Interviews

Dale Drury and Gabe Lenhart discuss nursing care and veteran benefits: http://www.seniorcareofsacramento.com/blog/dale-drury-interview-MediCal or Medicaid-skilled-nursing-entitlements-veterans-benefits/

Organizations and Institutional Resources

Veterans Administration

The 2016 Guide to Federal Benefits for Veterans Dependents and Survivors (76 pages) http://www.va.gov/opa/publications/benefits_book/2016_Federal_Benefits_for_Veterans.pdf

National Resource Directory: a guide to 17,000+ organized and vetted resources for service members, veterans, families, and military caregivers https://www.nrd.gov

Includes sections on Benefits & Compensation, Community of Care, Education and Training, Employment, Family and Care Giver Support, Health, Homeless Assistance, Housing, Transportation and Travel

Aid and Attendance Benefit http://www.benefits.va.gov/pension/aid_attendance_housebound.asp

The National Council on Aging (NCOA)

Explore the NCOA's benefits homepages https://www.ncoa.org/economic-security/benefits and https://www.benefitscheckup.org

The webpage has direct links to the NCOA's resource pages for Medicaid & Medicare Savings Programs, Medicare Advantage, Medicare and Dental Coverage, Medicare and Hearing, Medicare and Vision Coverage, Prescription

Assistance Programs, Energy Assistance Benefits, and the Supplemental Nutrition Assistance Program (SNAP).

NCOA Youtube Channel
https://www.youtube.com/user/ncoaging

NCOA Benefits Checkup web tool "See if you're eligible for benefits to pay for food, medicine, rent, and other daily expenses." https://www.benefitscheckup.org

Email a question to the NCOA https://www.ncoa.org/get-involved/contact-us/email

American Public Transportation Association Directory

http://www.apta.com

Area Agency on Aging or The Aging and Disability Resource Centers

BenefitsCheckup.org

Commodity Supplemental Food Program (CSFP)

Emergency Food Assistance Program TEFAP

Home Delivered Meals and Congregate Meals

Home Purchase Programs

HUD Programs

Legal Aid for the Elderly (legal services offices and hotline services)

Low-Income Subsidy (LIS) / Extra Help Prescription Assistance

Medicaid.gov/LTSS/Institutional

Medicare Savings Programs

National Aging and Disability Transportation Center

NADTC.ORG

Older Americans Act Title VI Programs and Services Title VI of The Older Americans Act (OAA) For Native Americans - Indian, Alaskan & Hawaii

Patient Assistance Programs (PAPS)

Property Tax Relief

Senior Farmers' Market Nutrition Program (SFMNP)

SNAP

Social Security Divorced Spouse Benefit

SSI Income, Tax and Legal Support

State-By-State 211 Information Lines

SHIP (State Health Insurance Assistance Programs) Resource Center

https://www.shiptacenter.org

Tax Counseling for the Elderly (TCE)

Temporary Assistance for Needy Families (TANF)

The Alzheimer's Association $1000 Respite Grant

The Emergency Food Assistance Program (TEFAP)

The National Association of Area Agencies on Aging (N4A)

The Senior Community Service Employment Program

Title VI Programs Run By Tribes or Native Groups

Weatherization Assistance Program (WAP)

The Following Pages Feature

Trusted Resources

That We Recommend

147

Divine Mercy Guest Home

**is the trusted and sought
after residential care facility
for the elderly.**

Phone:
916-487-3719

Address:
3180 Watt Avenue
Sacramento, California
95821

Will I run out of Money?

Individualized detailed income and expense analysis projected over 50 years. Knowledge is power. Get the answers now. Know exactly where you stand.

This is not a calculator which is an over simplification. This is a personalized report based on your circumstances that lays out a column for every year of your future.

✓ Income and expenses projected with varying return and inflation rates. For example, the cost of a dishwasher when you are 82. Yearly asset balance.
✓ Factors in overlooked expenses ie. re-roofing, major appliance replacements, routine maintenance, septic pumping every 5 years, lawn help at 65, full gardener at 70, housecleaner at 65, assisted living at 85/90 (at age when you say), conversion from health insurance to medicare, medigap...and more down to manicures, adjusted every year at varying inflation rates.
✓ Your plan will vary every year because of a new car, dishwasher, European vacation, etc.
✓ What if's like when to retire/take social security, sell home, sell rentals, convert CD's to annuities, etc.
✓ On the right path or do you have to ramp it up, change investment strategies, prepare to work longer, etc.
✓ *Most reports $325. Slightly higher w/rentals.*
✓ **A must for anyone over 50**

Cynthia Comiskey
Financial Analyst
email: willirunoutofmoney@gmail.com
website: willirunoutofmoney.us
(916) 663-9090

155

About The Author

Therese Johnson is a freelance, International Magazine and online writer, newspaper and e-book author as well as a local TV producer, Radio show host for "Senior Moments" on 105.5 FM and the founder of Senior Care of Sacramento. She is a gerontologist, community and social service specialist, continuing education provider, and administrator for residential care facilities for the elderly (RCFE). She is an Alzheimer's specialist and certified nurse's assistant. Therese is passionate about optimizing the quality of life for senior citizens, through taking an integrative medicine approach to their care, as well as engaging in social and financial advocacy on their behalf. Therese has spent the last 18 years working in acute care, long-term care, and residential care for the elderly. While serving as the president and legislative advocate of Foothill Association of Care Providers for the Elderly (FACES), Therese sponsored and successfully passed the California "Assisted Living Waiver Pilot Project", requiring Medi-Cal to fund RCFES and Board and Care - small, home-like environments offering seniors personalized attention, private quarters, and dignified lifestyles. Prior to the passage of this bill, California Medi-Cal only funded skilled nursing facilities.

For more information about Saving Seniors' Savings, please visit www.SavingSeniorsSavings.com, or contact www.SeniorCareofSacramento.com or call 916-877-6904.